THE PRAYER WAY
TO HEALTH,
WEALTH, AND HAPPINESS

Also by Lowell Fillmore

(out of print)

Remember

New Ways to Solve Old Problems

Things to Be Remembered

The Unity Treasure Chest:
   A Selection of the Best of Unity Writing,
   compiled by Lowell Fillmore

THE PRAYER WAY TO HEALTH, WEALTH, AND HAPPINESS

LOWELL FILLMORE

Foreword
by James Dillet Freeman

Unity Classic Library

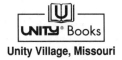

UNITY® Books

Unity Village, Missouri

The Prayer Way to Health, Wealth, and Happiness is a member of the Unity Classic Library.

The Unity Classic Library is guided by the belief of Unity cofounder Charles Fillmore that "whatever God has revealed to man in one age He will continue to reveal to him in all ages." The series projects Fillmore's vision of Unity as "a link in the great educational movement inaugurated by Jesus Christ" to help and teach humankind to use and prove eternal Truth.

To receive a catalog of all Unity publications (books, cassettes, compact discs, and magazines) or to place an order, call the Customer Service Department: (816) 969-2069 or 1-800-669-0282. For information, address Unity Books, Publishers, Unity School of Christianity, 1901 NW Blue Parkway, Unity Village, MO 64065-0001.

First edition 1964; fifth printing 1991
Second edition 2000

Marbled design by Mimi Schleicher © 1994
Cover design by Jill L. Ziegler

Library of Congress Cataloging-in-Publication Data
Fillmore, Lowell, b. 1882.
　The prayer way to health, wealth, and happiness / Lowell
　　Fillmore.
　　　p.　　cm.
　ISBN 0-87159-255-X (alk. paper)
　1. Christian life—Unity School of Christianity authors.　2.
Unity School of Christianity—Doctrines.　3. Prayer—Unity
School of Christianity.　I. Title.
BX9890.U505F59　　　2000
248.4'8997—dc21　　　　　　　　　　　　　　99-36564
　　　　　　　　　　　　　　　　　　　　　　　　　　CIP

Canada BN 13252 9033 RT

"The whole world is waiting for you and me to express our unity with God's love. Let us no longer think, 'Let somebody else start the millennium, and I will try to follow him.' Everyone who reads this may start a new spiritual wave of peace on earth today if he will begin now to practice loving God all day long every day. This great opportunity is waiting for any person who is willing to make a business of loving God. By expressing each day more love to God you will discover that love is the key that unlocks the door to God's kingdom."

Lowell Fillmore

Contents

Foreword

Remember to smile.

Remember to say a good word.

Remember to remember only the good.

These are the opening words of a column that appeared for the first time in the March 12, 1910, issue of a magazine that was then only a few months old.

The name of the magazine is *Weekly Unity*.

The name of the column is "Things to Be Remembered."

The name of the writer is Lowell Page Fillmore.

Since then, week in, week out, continuously, never missing a single issue, Lowell Fillmore has written almost three thousand "Things to Be Remembered" columns. But those opening words of that first column are still the basis—as they were the basis then—of the life of this man who, in this diamond-jubilee year of Unity, at eighty-two, is president and manager of Unity School of Christianity.

If you ransacked all the dictionaries for words to describe Lowell Fillmore, you could find none more fitting than those he himself chose so long ago. If today you encountered this twinkle-eyed man—writing at his desk in the big front office room of the Administration Building at Unity Village, or going from table to table at lunchtime in Unity Inn to exchange greetings with his fellow workers, or speaking in a Unity center where he has come to dedicate a building, or presiding at a board meeting that he has called to decide Unity's course, or planting new varieties of plants in his garden—you would probably find him smiling. Even more certainly, you would find him trying to get those around him to smile.

And if you asked his friends and fellow workers to describe him with a single word, I believe the word every one of them would think of first is *good*—and they might add, "He has a good word for everyone."

Lowell Fillmore wrote his first "Things to Be Remembered" more than half a century ago. But that is not when he began to work for Unity. When he began to work for Unity, he almost cannot remember.

Lowell Fillmore was born January 4, 1882, in Pueblo, Colorado. The year usually given as the start of Unity is 1889, when Charles and Myrtle Fillmore brought out the first issue of *Modern Thought*, a name they shortly changed to *Unity*. This year, 1964, marks the seventy-fifth anniversary of that event.

It was in 1886 in Kansas City, where the Fillmores had moved two years before, that his mother went to a lecture by Dr. E. B. Weeks. There she had the realization, "I am a child of God and therefore I do not inherit sickness," that was to heal her body, electrify her thought, and transform her life. Lowell was barely four years old.

From that moment on, the life of Lowell Fillmore—along with the lives of how many millions of other people!—was never to be the same again. From that moment on, the life of Lowell Fillmore was to be summed up in one word: *Unity*.

"I was not more than four or five years old," Lowell has said, "when I remember my mother helping others. The first person I remember was an old Irishman. He lived across the street from us out on Wabash, and he was crippled and had to walk on crutches.

"This was just shortly after Mother had been healed and had begun helping her neighbors. Anyhow, this Irishman, whose name was Caskey, came to Mother. She would tell him to put his crutches down and walk, and he would say, 'How do I know I can walk?' But Mother would keep working with him until he finally put down his crutches and walked across the room. When I saw him several years later, he was driving an express wagon, and he jumped down off it and shook my hand. He was just like a young fellow."

While Lowell was still in grade school, he would go down to the rooms in the Hall Building on Saturdays and help wrap the magazines. His father would pay him ten cents for this.

His mother would read to him the stories she was writing for *Wee Wisdom*. Sometimes Lowell would tell her, "Boys don't say it that way," but when she had finished the stories, he cried out to her, "Oh, Mama, please write more; nobody can tell it like Aunt Joy or write like Trixie."

Almost his earliest memories are of meetings he attended, led by his father on the fifth floor of the Hall Building in downtown Kansas City. He and his younger brother "Rick"—Waldo Rickert Fillmore, born in 1884—loved to hang out of the window and stare down at the people far below and at the cable cars that crawled up and down the steep hill. To the meetings would come, Lowell has said, "bearded metaphysicians with heavy golden watch chains across their fancy vests, and women in huge flowered hats who sometimes came to listen to Father and sometimes to speak themselves."

Sometimes in those early years, the family did not have much money. "We wore shiny clothes," Lowell has said, "but we got by." It was not only their clothes that shone, it was their faces and their spirits. Life glowed, if not with money, with the golden coin of laughter.

When he finished high school, Lowell went to

work for Unity at five dollars a week, which, he said, "I considered a tremendous sum of money."

By the time he was in his teens, he was helping on Sundays by teaching Sunday school. "I had about ten students," he said. "They were almost as old as I was."

When Unity moved into a rented house on McGee Street, a small job press was set up in the kitchen. "This," said Lowell, "I used to run. When I worked in the evenings and wanted to clean the press, I would have to turn out the gaslights and do it in the dark, so that the gasoline I used would not cause an explosion. We couldn't have a fire in the stove for the same reason. Sometimes in the winter it got pretty cold."

When the work was in the house on McGee Street, Lowell recalls: "Many things that I did as a part of the daily routine and that took me just a few minutes to do alone constitute whole departments now. I ran the job press, printed the envelopes and stationery, and helped write the letters. When the type was taken from our office, I would help load up the forms, take them to a commercial press-room—not ours—and help unload them; then after the magazines were printed, I would help mail them.

"We would buy wrapping paper in big sheets, and had a cutter in the back room. I would cut the wrappers to the proper length, fasten them to the desk with a clamp, and then address them with the Dick mailer.

"We hung copies of this mailing list upstairs on a closet door, and that was our subscription and 'look-up' department. Every time we got a new subscription, we would write the name on the bottom of the list."

At that time *Lessons in Truth* was not a book, but a set of booklets. It was one of Lowell's jobs to sew the backs on these booklets with yarn of various colors, tying a bow in the middle.

"I was also the order-filling department. I often found that we were out of some of our books, which had been printed but not yet folded or bound. So I would go and get the printed sheets of paper, fold them by hand, get them ready, and stitch them and trim them. We kept our finished stock in the office in the front room; the printed pages, covers, binding materials, and other things, in the pantry of the old house. I would wrap and stamp the books and take them to the post office. Often my brother Rick would take them in his pony cart. We [took] time-out to mow the lawn and run errands."

The typewriter was a recent invention. Lowell learned the touch system. Also he learned shorthand, and occasionally took down the lectures his father gave.

For many years there were few to do the many

chores that had to be done. But there was always one whom Charles and Myrtle Fillmore could depend on to put his mind—and his shoulder, if need be—to any chore, no matter how arduous or irksome it might seem.

Often Lowell felt ill-prepared to do the things that were asked of him. But he knew that usually there was no one else to do them except him. So he did them.

One day, when the man who had been managing the business office left, his father called him in and told him, "Lowell, you are going to have to be the businessman."

A lad in his early twenties, self-effacing, timid, shy about meeting people, he suddenly found himself thrust into a position where he was going to have to make decisions, meet people constantly, take a large measure of responsibility, and give orders.

"At first I thought I couldn't do it," he said. "But Father told me I was the only one available, and I knew I always had recourse to prayer. So I went ahead."

Go ahead, he did—and Unity went ahead with him. When the Unity Society of Practical Christianity was organized, he was on the first Board of Directors—and he still is on the Board of Directors. He taught in the Sunday school, served as superintendent, helped his parents with Sunday service.

When a new magazine, *Weekly Unity*, was brought out in 1909, he was the first editor—and he has been the editor continuously since it started. In 1910 he began to write his "Remembers." He has written three books of articles and a little book of verse.

When in 1910 the building was erected at 917 Tracy Avenue that was to be the home of Unity School for the next forty years, his was a principal hand in its planning. When the work was moved to Unity Village, he was one of the leaders in that move, too. In 1933 when his father, in order to travel and write, began to relinquish active command of Unity, it was to Lowell Fillmore that he gave the reins. And when Charles Fillmore passed on in 1948 (Lowell was at his father's bedside), Lowell Fillmore became president of Unity School of Christianity.

Unity and Lowell Fillmore have had not two lives, but one. To serve God, to serve good—this has been his reason for being. There has been no job too small for him to apply his energy to; there has been no job too large for him to undertake.

Ask him what he does, and he answers: "I don't do anything. The rest of the people do the work around here."

This man who "does not do anything" comes to work early each Monday morning, usually getting to his desk before 7:30 a.m. He leaves in the evening long after the ordinary time for quitting, which is 5 p.m.

Through the week, when he does not have someone at his desk, he is busy with the voluminous correspondence he carries on with many famous and near-famous people throughout the world. He tries to read and answer personally the letters of all persons who have been Unity students for twenty years or longer. Also, he has his weekly "Remember" to write. Sometimes he writes out this column by hand; sometimes he dictates it and then rewrites his first rendition.

The first thing every Monday morning he conducts a meeting, during which he delivers a twenty-minute speech and leads the Unity workers in their *Daily Word* meditation.

Speaking has never come easily for Lowell, but like his father, he has gone on lecture tours and has dedicated Unity centers in many places.

He rarely leaves Unity School, however. "I don't need a vacation," Lowell says. "My vocation is my vacation."

Retta Chilcott, who has worked at his side for fifty years and is Unity's office manager, says, "I never remember Lowell staying home, not even for half a day."

A big man, he has always had extraordinary vigor. He is rarely seen walking upstairs—he runs up them two steps at a time. A friend told me that many years ago when they all lived together at Unity Farm, Lowell would take off his shoes and stockings and run barefoot in the winter snow—just out of exhilaration, out of the joy of being alive.

Lowell lives with his wife in a tranquil, hillside house in Unity Village. On February 14, 1926—Valentine's Day—Lowell married Alice Lee, who had worked at Unity School for several years. They had no children, but shortly after their marriage, they took into their home Lowell's niece Frances (the daughter of his youngest brother Royal, who passed on in 1923). Frances made her home with Alice and Lowell until she graduated from college. She is now Mrs. Robert Lakin, and has three children.

At his home, Lowell engages in the only interest outside of Unity that he has ever had. Lowell is a gardener.

When he was a boy, he filled his parents' yard with flowers. He built a greenhouse there where he could grow plants.

Today, at eighty-two, he cares for an acre of plants. There are few varieties of flowers or vegetables that at some time or other he has not grown.

Lowell Fillmore is one of the easiest men in the world to meet. He does not even have a private office. Dressed in neat but plain clothing, he sits at a desk in a corner of a large room on the ground floor of the Unity Administration Building, to the right of the main entrance. Behind him are banks of books. Alongside him are filing cabinets. On top of one of these he has a collection of tiny figurines and animal figures that people have sent him from all parts of the globe. Any visitor can walk freely up to Lowell's desk and introduce himself. To all of them he is simply "Lowell." Few workers ever address him in any other way.

Unassuming, free, thoughtful of others, ready to exchange the latest funny story or to discuss some profound metaphysical theme as the occasion demands, Lowell Fillmore is "just folks."

Almost every day he eats lunch with the other workers in Unity Inn. From childhood he has been a strict vegetarian, but he has never insisted that anyone else be. In the Inn he may join any worker beside whom there is an empty seat. It is not unusual for the newest worker at Unity to hear someone ask, "Do you mind if I eat with you?" When he looks up, that someone is the president of Unity School.

Unity Inn is a cafeteria. Lowell Fillmore takes his place in the line like any one of the workers; after lunch, he carries back his tray of dishes. Then he usually goes from table to table, usually with a new joke to tell.

Where there is laughter, there Lowell is likely to be. "Remember to smile," he wrote, and this is a smiling man. His speeches tingle with jokes, quips, and puns. "The pun," he once said, "is the Lowell-est form of humor."

Unity believes that when joy is put back into religion, there will be more religion in the world. Lowell has done his best to put joy into his religion.

In the early 1900s when the first Unity youth group was organized, it was called the "Joyful Circle." Lowell was one of its first members. For many years he took charge of all Unity picnics and parties, and Unity has put on few entertainments where the name of Lowell Fillmore has not appeared among the list of characters.

End man in a minstrel show, washerwoman singing Irish songs, schoolteacher, schoolboy, preacher, scarecrow, Harry Lauder singing Scotch ballads—Lowell has been all of these and scores of other characters.

Two years ago at the annual banquet for Unity center leaders, Lowell, with a pillow stuffed in his patched trousers, stole the show as Charlie Weaver. The performance was such good fun that he was asked to repeat it at Christmas for the Unity workers.

Christmas is a joyous time at Unity headquarters. Every year it reaches its climax when Lowell dons the familiar red suit and white beard of Santa Claus and goes among the hundreds of workers at Unity School to shake the hand of every one of them and give each one a special blessing. Lowell insists on greeting each one personally. "These are the hands that do the work," he says.

Unity teaches the power of positive thinking. Lowell Fillmore practices it.

"He never agrees with negation," says Retta Chilcott. "Many times through the years, when some disturbing incident has occurred at the office, when someone has fallen sick or some inharmony has arisen, I have turned to Lowell. I have always found him understanding of people and their needs, but I have always found him standing firm on his faith."

This he has done for himself, too. A few years ago Lowell caught his hand in an electric fan. When friends took him to a doctor, the doctor wanted to cut off one of his fingers which had been almost completely severed. "No," Lowell said firmly. "Put the finger back." Today the hand is completely whole.

When Lowell is called on to help with a problem, he becomes very still, his face a concentration in tranquility. He folds his hands in front of him, and there they rest, motionless. To see him is to know that here is a man who through a long life has practiced the art of meditation, whose first thought is always one of going to God.

Take a problem to Lowell Fillmore, and you may find the answer to your problem not in anything he says, but in the man himself. Instead of going into the negative details of your problem, he is likely to get you looking at the new figurines someone has sent him. Or he may talk to you about the flowers he is raising. Or he may show you some unusual vegetable he has brought to the office. After a while, you may find that his undisturbed detachment has transferred itself into you.

"Minimize the problem; magnify the Lord," he has said.

This is a man of great faith.

Retta Chilcott tells how "when the work on the building at 917 Tracy started, we did not have any funds on hand for the purpose; but we started to put up the building, and through faith and prayer we demonstrated enough funds each week to meet our bills and our payroll, which we took care of each Saturday. Sometimes even as late as Saturday morning Lowell Fillmore would come to our desks and remind us that we had the payroll and bills for material to meet that day and that we needed more funds. 'We must pray about it,' he would say. So far as I know it was not necessary for us to borrow money at a bank or anywhere else to meet those obligations."

When it was decided to build Unity Temple in Kansas City, Lowell Fillmore was chosen to head the building committee. A lot was purchased at 47th and Jefferson, where the Temple is now located. Then came World War II, which halted all plans. When the war ended, the project went forward again. The excavation was dug and the foundation poured.

It had been expected that the Temple would cost perhaps as much as $600,000, and this seemed a huge sum to everyone.

Then one Friday night in 1946, an official for the construction company appeared before the committee. "This Temple will not cost $600,000," he told them. "It will cost at least $1,000,000."

Silent consternation fell over the group. For several minutes, as each person tried to absorb the full meaning of this shattering announcement, no one uttered a syllable. The sum of $600,000 had seemed a huge amount to undertake to raise. Now, $1,000,000!

Slowly all eyes turned toward Lowell Fillmore, the chairman of the committee. He had been sitting quietly with his eyes closed, as is his custom. Now he opened his eyes, looked at the group, and spoke these words: "We shall go ahead!"

A few minutes later the meeting adjourned and the group filed out. But ringing in the minds of all of them were the firm words of faith: "We shall go ahead!" Go ahead, they did. The Temple was built. It was paid for.

In his first days at Unity, Charles Fillmore had told his son, "You are to be the businessman." When Lowell was a boy, it was up to him to keep the

financial records and bank accounts; he signed the
checks. Before he became president of Unity
School, he was treasurer. He is a practical man—he
originated the Prosperity Bank, one of the most
helpful and popular ideas conceived at Unity—but
he has run Unity's business in a way that few busi-
nessmen might recognize as businesslike.

Barney Ricketts, present treasurer of Unity
School and head of the Accounting Department for
thirty-five years, says of Lowell Fillmore, "He
comes nearer to living up to what he sees to be the
Truth than anyone I know."

Unity gives away tremendous quantities of literature. It sends thousands of pieces of literature to
hospitals, prisons, and other institutions. It pub-
lishes in Braille for the blind. In fact, it gives its
magazines and books to anyone who says he cannot
afford to pay for them.

"The Lord will take care of His workers," Lowell
has said, "if His workers just take care of His work."

Though almost no money comes to Unity from
foreign countries, Lowell has kept the literature
flowing freely into them.

He originated a Spanish-language magazine. He
promoted publication of *Daily Word* in the many
languages in which it is now printed. He has
encouraged the translation of books and pamphlets.
He has personally carried on a correspondence with

interested persons in dozens of countries. He has even studied Spanish.

Among his proudest possessions are two beautifully hand-bound books. They contain his "Remembers," all carefully typed—in English on one page, in Spanish on the opposite page. A woman teacher in Mexico City made the books and used them as a means of teaching English.

Today scores of thousands of persons in strange and far-off places—in the bush country of Nigeria, in Finland, in the islands of the Caribbean Sea, in the countries of Latin America, in India and Japan, in Germany and Italy and France, and many other places—receive the Unity message because of the faith of Lowell Fillmore.

"If you want to get Lowell to do something," Barney Ricketts has said, "you don't tell him how much it will cost or how much money it will bring in; you tell him how much good it is going to do. In all the years I have worked with him, I have never seen Lowell make a decision on any other basis than that of service. 'How many people will it bless?' This is the question he asks."

He takes the same attitude toward Unity's workers that he takes toward Unity's finances. When a change is suggested in the work, his first question is likely to be, "Can this be done without hurting anyone?"

Those who work close to him say that when you have to tell him unhappy things about a worker, he never agrees with you. He is kind in the estimates he makes of people. He looks for the good in them.

As God's businessman conducting God's business, Lowell Fillmore has been coordinator of the practical and the spiritual activities of Unity for more than thirty years. During this period of his direction, Unity has made tremendous growth. The work has moved from its old headquarters on Tracy Avenue to the beautiful setting and buildings at Unity Village. The circulation of the magazines has more than doubled. Unity has entered the fields of radio and television—today more than seventy stations carry the *Unity Viewpoint* radio program; another seventy stations carry the *Daily Word* television program. Where thirty years ago there was only a handful of Unity centers, today there are almost three hundred. Where there was almost no foreign work at all, today Unity is spreading rapidly around the world.

Lowell Fillmore has proved that gentle goodness is also good business.

There is a legend told about a saint. He was such a good man that an angel came to him and told him God would grant any wish he asked. The saint said, "Whenever my shadow falls behind me as I walk, may whatever it falls on be blessed."

When I was asked to write about Lowell Fillmore, I talked with many people who had been associated with him in the Unity work. I was trying to find stories about Lowell as a person. But after a time I discovered an interesting thing. Instead of telling me stories about Lowell, these people were soon telling me stories about themselves—about the effect that Lowell Fillmore had had on their lives, about how Lowell's devotion to principle, Lowell's simplicity, Lowell's modesty, Lowell's goodness had influenced them to be the kind of persons they were and to do the work they had done for Unity.

When people think of Lowell Fillmore, they do not think of shining anecdotes and glittering personal exploits; they think only of the influence he has (quietly, impersonally, subtly as if it were his shadow) cast on their lives.

Once Lowell Fillmore said to a friend: "If anyone gets to thinking he is great, let him go down to the water's edge and thrust his hand into the water. Then let him pull his hand out again, and see how much of an impression he leaves."

Lowell Fillmore is like water. Ask me to tell what water is like and all that I can say is that it quenches my thirst.

More than fifty-four years ago, Lowell Fillmore wrote his first "Things to Be Remembered." He wrote:

Remember to smile.

Remember to say a good word.

Remember to remember only the good.

Of Lowell Fillmore, it is enough to say, "He has remembered."

—*James Dillet Freeman*
1964

Preface

During my many years of activity in the work of Unity School of Christianity, I have had the happy privilege of writing, under the inspiration of the Spirit of Truth, hundreds of Truth articles, occasional poems, and miscellaneous bits of spiritual philosophy. Many letters come to Unity from readers who testify to the help that they have derived from using the ideas that I have sought to explain in my writings.

A number of years ago, Unity printed on a card "Metaphysical Gadgets," a group of thirteen Truth affirmations that I compiled after having proved their spiritual worth in my own life. Users tell me that they have found these gadgets valuable in meeting everyday problems involving health, prosperity, and human relationships.

Each chapter of this book, except that on the Lord's Prayer, is based on one of the gadgets.

—*Lowell Fillmore*
1964

The Answer

When for a purpose
I had prayed and prayed and prayed
Until my words seemed worn and bare
    With arduous use,
And I had knocked and asked and knocked and
        asked again,
And all my fervor and persistence brought no
        hope,
I paused to give my weary brain a rest
And ceased my anxious human cry.
    In that still moment,
After self had tried and failed,
There came a glorious vision of God's power,
And, lo, my prayer was answered in that hour.
                                    —*Lowell Fillmore*

Chapter 1

The Positive Outlook

I go to meet my good.

Heaven Is Here

FOR many years good Christians have been praying for the kingdom to come into the earth, but they have always thought of it as coming at an undetermined future date. I believe it is time to do something more definite concerning the coming of the kingdom. I believe Jesus Christ meant for man to enjoy it now, for He often said that it was at hand. By concerted effort and faithful practice I feel sure that a group of faithful Christians can bring the kingdom of heaven into the earth now, at the present time.

The kingdom of heaven does not come by observation, but it must be incorporated into our life by actual practice and work. It will be the purpose of our club to begin this work at once. Its members will be those who agree to cooperate in meeting each little daily problem in a simple but effective way, which I will now try to point out.

While I believe it is possible for one person to find the kingdom alone, I am sure that it will be easier for each one if a number of persons will join together in a united effort. There will be no membership record kept of the Heaven Is Here Club. Each one desiring to join will simply make a covenant with the Father. Membership dues will consist of the effort the member puts into work to be done.

The first thing for a member to realize is that heaven is not a place far distant but that it is a harmonious state of mind that each member must endeavor to establish in himself.

The kingdom of heaven is man's true estate. God made man perfect in the beginning. This perfect man lives in the kingdom of heaven now. When you realize your unity with God and that you, the real you, are a son of God you will begin to see that the kingdom of heaven is truly at hand.

Heaven is here waiting to be called into expression in our life. We must begin by calling it into expression in every little experience. We can practice bringing heaven into the earth every minute of the day. We can practice upon the conditions that come into our life.

As Adam named the animals, we can name these conditions, giving them heavenly names. The events of life are passing by us endlessly, and we are naming some of them bad and some good. It seems strange that all men do not agree, but some call certain things good that others call bad. This shows that the good and bad qualities exist in the minds of individuals and not in the things themselves. Here is an example:

Fifty years ago short skirts were said to be bad by most persons in this country, but today they are called good by the majority. This change of name from bad to good is entirely in the mind of the people. Shakespeare expresses it in these words: "There is nothing either good or bad, but thinking makes it so."

Let each member of our club realize that what he thinks about a thing or an experience is more important than the thing or experience itself. Suppose you dread to meet someone with whom you have an appointment and you anticipate an unpleasant interview. Here is an opportunity to practice the presence of the kingdom of heaven. Say silently: "There are no unpleasant experiences in heaven, which is now here; therefore I go fearlessly to meet my good." This thought will take you to the appointment with your mind free from fear and bitterness. You will have a light heart and will very likely wear a smile on your face, which will send a signal to the other person that the interview is to be a pleasant one.

Remember that because the interview is to be held in the kingdom, only pleasant things will be discussed. As you see goodness and light like a cloud all about you both, you will realize that the kingdom of heaven is dominating that conversation whether the other person realizes it or not, and you will both enjoy and receive benefits from the meeting. Do not allow yourself to think for a minute that anything but good can come from it.

If a member of your family seems not to be co-operating with the others, stop accenting thoughts of criticism concerning him and think heavenly thoughts instead of dark thoughts about him. It is so easy when you are in the earthly state of mind to whine and feel sorry for yourself.

But this is not the way things are done in the kingdom of heaven. Remember that you are in the kingdom and be cheerful. Say to yourself: "Order is heaven's first law. In the kingdom of heaven all is divine order. Everybody is loving and kind." Do not admit to yourself that there is any other possibility. Stick to this thought. Put your will in the background and allow the will of God to be done in this matter and believe in the presence of the kingdom so completely that its beauty will envelop the household, causing all of its members to cooperate perfectly.

If someone has been untrue to you, do not mourn about it but remember that there is no mourning in the kingdom of heaven, for heaven is founded upon joy. Forgive the person who seems to be untrue to you and think of him as a perfect child of God. Do not condemn him, but in your thoughts set him free to express his true nature in the kingdom. Know that all is well in the kingdom of heaven, where you both now reside. Be willing to admit that your ideas as well as his may need adjusting to conform to the standard of the kingdom.

It may be possible that you too need to ask forgiveness. Assume the heavenly attitude until you feel perfectly harmonious and happy. Having forgiven the "untrue" person, you will be able to understand that nothing unpleasant can happen in the kingdom.

If you have a decision to make that has been troubling you, place the matter in God's hands and realize that His wisdom is guiding you. Remember that God's wisdom is greater than man's knowledge and that He is showing you just what to do. There is no use to worry about anything that you have placed in His hands. Retain this attitude until you feel happy in the faith that all is well. Do not doubt God's wisdom; do not fear the outcome. Carry the kingdom of heaven with you into your decision. Remember that no unfair man-made law can withstand the goodness of the kingdom.

In dealing with your other experiences, remember that you are still in the kingdom and that you have taken all your affairs there with you. Surround yourself with a spiritual radiance, which will assure you that the kingdom of heaven is indeed now on your earth.

When you remember that there are many other members of the club working with you for the kingdom, you will not fail them. If you should be unable to bring one of your problems into the kingdom, do not worry but pull yourself together and try again, resolving to do better next time. And when you go to bed at night after a day of living in the kingdom, do not forget that you are still in heaven and that you will go into dreamland with a consciousness that you are going to spend the night in the kingdom, and I promise you that you will have a delightful and restful sleep.

The foregoing are but a few suggestions as to how you can practice bringing the kingdom of heaven into a few of your experiences. The same general plan can be adjusted to fit every kind of experience. Try faithfully for one day to bring the kingdom into your affairs, and I feel certain that you will want to continue the experiment indefinitely. Keep it up for a month and see how it will transform your affairs.

Remember that the kingdom of heaven is within you. Claim it. Live it. Enjoy it every day and every minute of every day.

Look for the Best

Everyone devotes a good deal of time to seeing with his mind's eye either the good things that he would like to attain or the unpleasant things that he would like to avoid. His mind may flit about pleasantly for a time among good things and then dart into the shadows of disturbing things, and once in a while it may find itself held spellbound by some possibility that terrifies it.

The pictures in our mind, whether they be pleasant, disturbing, or terrifying, are the charts of our future life course. If we are picturing good, happy things, we are charting a pleasant journey for the future. Because our mental picture may concern a present experience, we must learn to make our mental picture good even when our present experience seems to be bad. We can do this by seeing God as Spirit present in every experience and greater than the outer aspect of it.

It is an interesting fact that we usually run into the thing we are looking at. That is, we run into the condition that we have our mind fixed on. Many years ago I had an uncle who was learning to ride a bicycle, and he remarked how strange it was that he ran into whatever he was looking at. If he fixed his gaze upon a telephone pole he was sure to run into it. I have often thought how well his experience illustrates our own experiences, how we run into just the pleasant or unpleasant situation in life that we consider.

For example, I may have a problem, or at least it may seem to be a problem to me, and I may wish to solve it through prayer. I do not want the conditions of my problem to continue as they are, but they do continue because I keep my mind on them instead of turning it toward the pictures of peace, harmony, and good that exist in God's kingdom. I do not wish to have my problem persist, but I want instead the conditions of harmony, peace, good will, and success that are in the kingdom.

If I address a prayer to God but keep my attention on the problem, I shall therefore still have my problem. I am going to run into my problem and keep running into it as long as I keep my attention upon it. My need is to fix my attention upon the omnipresence of God's goodness so that I will run into that heavenly condition.

Are you facing a problem now? If so, are you fixing your attention upon the power of God to bring good into your life or are you fixing your main thought upon the reality of your problem? Your thoughts may run something like this: "Yes, I know that God is omnipresent, and omnipotent, and that He is good; but what am I going to do when the rent is due and I am likely to be evicted from my home because I have no money to pay?" This is a statement of your problem. Get your mind off it long enough so that you can see another picture, the picture of God's power. If the problem before you is the great thing and God is merely the "little helper" off to one side, how can He help you? Keep your eyes on the reality of the problem and you keep in the rut.

Is someone persecuting you or does someone in the family misunderstand your motives? Is there a wayward member in your family? If there is, do not fix your attention upon his waywardness and hope to cure it by merely saying, "O God, won't you help this situation?" If there were a beam balance that showed whether your thoughts were on God's side or on your problem's side, you would see that those on your problem far outweigh those on the power of God!

Now take your mind off these unpleasant things and put your trust in God, giving thanks because He is omnipresent, omnipotent, and omniscient in spite of all appearances, and you will find a solution. Magnify God in your mind instead of magnifying negative ideas, and your problem will be solved. Doing this is about the most difficult thing the metaphysician has to do, yet it is the most necessary thing to do.

We are told to magnify the Lord, which simply means that we must increase our appreciation and understanding of and our trust in the Lord instead of magnifying our difficulties. Look for the best and magnify it, and you will be continually running into the best.

The higher you look, the farther you can see. You can see only a few feet when you look down; when you look straight ahead, you can see much farther, sometimes several miles; but when you look up you can see stars which are millions of miles away.

The higher we seek our ideals, the farther we shall see mentally. One who looks down into the material world for his ideals will understand only a little of the wonders of life. One who lifts his ideals to the great men about him will have a much larger appreciation of life, but one who lifts his ideal to the Christ opens for himself a mental and spiritual vision which is unlimited.

When we look at the stars and understand the vastness that is between them and us, we are able to appreciate the littleness of the cares that beset us in the daily round of life. If we do not look at the stars, the little things seem too big to bear. When we realize the wonders of the Christ perfection, we are able to see that the cares and worries of life are but little problems which can be solved easily by the use of spiritual law.

I Go to Meet My Good

The waking time of nearly every person is spent in association with other people.

We meet other people at home, in the street, in the air, on the train, on the ocean, in offices, in the market, and wherever we go. If there were no people about us, we would be very unhappy.

How we behave toward others determines what life means to us. Our attitude toward others can bring us happiness or unhappiness, but whether or not we find joy in living depends upon how we treat others rather than upon how they treat us. We meet all kinds of people in our world. Some of the people we meet may seem to us to be helpful and friendly, while others may seem to be unfriendly and offensive. The truth of the matter is that the good or bad results of our association with the people we meet depend more upon how we think and act toward them than upon how they act toward us. Therefore, the good we receive is dependent upon how we act toward others rather than upon how they act toward us.

We should obey the laws of the land, of course, but there is a higher law that controls our life and affairs more definitely than all of the man-made laws. This higher law is greater than all man-made laws, and if people obeyed it, then there would not be a need for man-made laws. This higher law is stated by Jesus Christ in Matthew 7:12 (ASV). Here is how He words it: "All things therefore whatsoever ye would that men should do unto you, even so do ye also unto them: for this is the law and the prophets." When we obey this law, doing only good to others and dealing harmoniously with them in our thoughts, words, feelings, and deeds, we shall find our good coming to us in every experience of our life.

Sometimes we may be worried about some appointment that we are to fulfill with another person or a committee. We dread it, because we think we do not know how to meet the ideas of others that may be contrary to our own ideas and feelings. Instead of fearing this meeting of minds, we should realize that this appointment can be an opportunity for us to express the Golden Rule and thereby lift up the consciousness of all who are present.

God has given us His power of love to use in overcoming what is not right in such an appointment. We cannot make this overcoming by condemning or by opposing what we think is wrong in the other person's views. We should let the power of God's love, forgiveness, and harmony enter into our mind at the meeting, and when we do this, we shall find a righteous and good solution to the problem that we would not have dreamed could come out of it.

In Luke 22:29 (ASV) we read how Jesus made an appointment for His disciples. They had been wondering who would be greatest among them, and He told them that a good servant was greater than his master. He tried to show them that meekness and love can make a person greater than force and the power of dominion over others can make him. He said: "And I appoint unto you a kingdom, even as my Father appointed unto me, that ye may eat and drink at my table in my kingdom; and ye shall sit on thrones judging the twelve tribes of Israel." In these words Jesus was describing how superior is one who enters into the kingdom of God than is one of the rulers of the world who sits on an earthly throne. Jesus sits on a throne of spiritual love and understanding and does not count Himself greater than others.

So let us rejoice in all our associations with others as we let God help us find good in all our appointments. God has appointed us to enter His kingdom within, and thereby to be protected from the misunderstandings of the world as we sit on the powerful throne of righteousness. Therefore, let us go joyously toward all of our appointments.

Where Are You Looking?

A preceding section brings out the fact that we usually go where we are looking. If we look for our good in the world only, we are looking in the wrong direction because we are looking away from

God and concentrating our attention on material things.

When we realize the Truth that God is the source of all good, we shall begin to look to God for our good first instead of searching for it in the world. When we direct our attention to God first, and look to Him in Spirit for our good, we shall be seeking our good at its source.

It is true that God is everywhere present. He is even in the things of the world, but we cannot find Him in these things until we first find Him within our own spiritual Self.

God created all things good by His Word. This statement means that all His creations are His perfect ideas. When we look to God first, we shall be able to see the manifestations of His ideas in the things of the world about us.

God also created His idea of man in His own image and likeness. His idea of man is a perfect being who also has power to create by the power of his words and ideas. But when a man believes in both good and evil, he is likely, because of his mixed ideas, to create conditions in his life that are not in accord with God's ideas.

God's perfect spiritual idea of man is the reality that animates every man's body. When man does not believe in his divine origin, he wrongly visions his body as being less than perfect, not meeting the perfect standard of God's spiritual idea of man, and he thereby separates his body from its potential perfection that God idealized for it.

Jesus Christ came into the world to show us how we can unify the perfect Son-of-God idea in us with our body by lifting up our ideas about our body and thereby helping to bring it into accord with God's perfect spiritual idea of man. Jesus overcame the flesh by lifting up His body consciousness so that His idea of it became unified with the Christ Spirit of perfection. Whether we believe it or not, God's spiritual idea of man is the life and power that moves every one of us. When we seek only in the world for our good, our thoughts move away from, instead of toward, our good.

Our good actually comes from God in spiritual ideas. We mold these ideas into the conditions of our life by our thoughts. When we think good, true thoughts, they help us to meet our good in our every experience. When we think untrue thoughts, we mold or form conditions in our life that are not in harmony with God's perfect plan. Because the thoughts that formed them are not actually true, these creations will eventually pass away. When we let God's perfect ideas work freely through us, we shall be able to do the greater works that Jesus Christ promised that we would do through the Father abiding in us.

Jesus was humble enough to deny His human desires for worldly riches and honor. Because He denied them, He opened His being for God to work freely through Him.

When we forgive our enemies, we are taking a step toward exercising our dominion over wrong thinking by unselfishly letting God's love nature in us work through us to overcome the mistakes of the world.

When we begin to understand and to make practical use of Jesus Christ's teachings, we shall find that He is with us at all times and that we do not have to wait for Him to come to us at a future time. It is true that He will come again at any time to anyone who has faith, patience, and meekness enough to accept Him in Spirit and in Truth. To those who believe in Him and dwell with Him in Spirit, He gives eternal life. The true Christian spirit in a man includes his practical application of Jesus Christ's teachings and principles in controlling his mind and body.

Jesus taught us that we are all children of God, for He taught us to join Him in saying, "Our Father who art in heaven." He also taught us to pray that God's kingdom may come into the earth so that the earth shall become as it is in heaven. Jesus' teachings must be practiced by a true Christian every minute of the day. It is not enough for us to read about Christ in the Bible, and to go to church on Sunday. When we have faith that God is with us at all times and we always seek Christ's guidance first, we shall be on our way to meet our good wherever we are in His kingdom.

Men have judged their surroundings by appearances for so long that they seem to have lost the true, clear vision, which sees everything perfect in Spirit. They do not seem to comprehend that the kingdom of heaven does not come by observation. They seem to have forgotten the promise that all these things shall be added, after the kingdom and its righteousness have been found.

We must get into the consciousness of God as love, life, intelligence, substance, and harmony, everywhere present in Spirit; and we must dwell in this state of knowing, in spite of all appearances. This is true faith. When we realize that God is actually everywhere present in Spirit, as love, life, intelligence, substance, and harmony, we are in the master seat, from which we are able to direct and change appearances.

Call Out the Good

You, a child of God, need never surrender your spiritual authority and dominion because of any negative barrier that may be placed across your path.

You are more than you appear to be. There is more to you than body and mind. You are also

Spirit, and it is the Spirit in you that gives you authority over all things, including the beasts of the field as well as your own mind and body.

When you meet an obstacle in the outer world, do not take it too seriously, but remember that there is a Spirit in you, which is greater than any negative condition.

All things in the world are good, but when these things are used by man in a way that is not in accord with the divine plan, we call them evil. Never allow yourself to become entangled in their web of disorder by letting the so-called evil overshadow the good; stand still in your spiritual might, and have faith in Truth, and thus help to establish divine order. Call out the good in all these things by blessing them and realizing their inherent goodness. Be willing to change your mind if you have been wrong in your appraisal of any situation.

Two and two equals four. This statement is good because it is true, but the statement that two and two equals six is not good because it is not true, although all the figures that are a part of it are good. The twos and the six are good, but they are not arranged according to Truth. The conclusion is wrong, not the figures on which it is based.

So it is with things about us that we call evil. Each thing in itself is good, but when it is in wrong relationship with the others, we call it evil. It may sometimes happen that the arrangement of the things or factors in any situation is right but we have misunderstood it, and we call it evil. Therefore we should always be willing to admit it when we are mistaken. We should not quarrel with inharmonious conditions, because this negative attitude will only add to the inharmony and confusion. We should bring harmony into the situation by affirming the Truth that establishes divine order. Instead of quarreling with the statement, "Two plus two equals six," we do not become upset when we know that it is not true and that two plus two equals four.

If somebody should take something that belongs to you, do not sacrifice your spiritual dominion by thinking and acting on the low level of anguish, fear, and unhappiness, but stand firm on the high ground of your spiritual authority by knowing the Truth. Let us analyze the situation and see what is good in it. The thing that was taken is good, the person who took it is good in Spirit—even though he may not be fully aware of his goodness, and you are good.

The three elements of the problem are good, but they are not in divine order. This disorder we call stealing. You can establish divine order by knowing the Truth that God is the source of good things. Therefore in Truth nothing can be taken away from you, for everything belongs to God. Declare the Truth that God is your supply and that nothing can be taken away from you; you will then find that if this particular thing is not restored to you, nevertheless God's infinite supply will supply you with something better. The person who did the wrong is accountable to himself and to God for his wrongdoing, and will need to correct his mistake before he can establish divine order in his life. There is no need for you to become involved in his misdeeds by accepting their untruth as reality, and thus stepping down from your seat of divine dominion.

If someone has lied about you, do not stumble over their untruth; realize that in Spirit there is only Truth and righteousness in your world. Nobody can throw your affairs into confusion but you yourself, and when you are established in Truth you will not make this mistake.

If you think you have lost something, know that because the thing you have apparently lost belongs to God, it will find its rightful place. Realize that nothing is lost in Spirit. Do not admit that you have lost anything, and do not let this experience cause you to forget your spiritual dominion.

In Spirit all things are in divine order, and when you maintain your spiritual standard, everything about you will find its orderly place. If the thing you have apparently lost is not truly yours in divine order, but belongs somewhere else, it will find its place. In any event be assured always that nothing that really belongs to you can be taken away from you.

Do not be too quick to condemn a person for what you think is wrong with him, because by your condemnation you cause a disturbance in your environment which is not in accord with divine order. Send out your blessings in a spirit of forgiveness, and you will help God to bring conditions back into divine order. Even though this order may not be complete as far as the other person's affairs are concerned, you will be free from adverse entanglements.

If someone bears false witness against you, do not lose your spiritual dominion, but affirm the Truth that when God is for you, no one can be against you. Do not worry; stand firm in the consciousness of God's love, and freely forgive the one who has seemingly done wrong. Set him free from your belief in his error by forgiving him and asking God's blessing upon him.

There is good in everything, and that good will come out to meet you when the Spirit in you calls it out. You can call it out only when you stand firmly on the spiritual foundation of your oneness with Christ. If someone does something that is wrong, you can best deal with this problem by doing something which is good and generous, rather than by doing an act of retaliation, or by worrying about it, or getting angry, or fighting against it with words or physical force.

Sometimes you may find it good to take the stand that Jesus did when He said, "Suffer *it* now."

This does not mean that you are agreeing with the error involved, or that you are running away from your responsibility. It means that while you are speaking the Truth, you have faith enough to depend upon divine order to straighten the tangles out in God's good time. However, you must not fail to do your righteous part while you are waiting. You may at times have to wait for others to grow better, but you should do your best now.

If you do something that is out of order, you should correct it at once if possible. You must be righteous and sincere, loving, kind, and willing at all times to change your mind if you have misjudged someone or misunderstood a situation, and be willing to accept the true facts.

All things are good, but when these good things are pushed out of order by human ignorance, they may seem to be evil. The Spirit of Christ in man is the saving power that can bring them back into divine order.

I go to meet my good.

A Prayer Drill

First Day. *The power of God fills my life with glory, adjusting all my problems.*

Second Day. *I am not fooled by adverse appearances, for I can see God's love shining through them.*

Third Day. *Visions of good are leading me into pleasant and prosperous ways, and all my paths are peaceful.*

Fourth Day. *My appreciation of God's power and goodness grows larger day by day as my troubles grow smaller.*

Fifth Day. *I magnify God by thinking often of the reality of His unbounded love, goodness, power, and wisdom.*

Sixth Day. *I look ever toward the light, and the shadows all fall behind me.*

Seventh Day. *All dark places are made light through my vision of Christ.*

Chapter 2

Life and Truth

My heart is right with God.

The Truth About You

THE most interesting subject that a man can study is himself. Realizing this, the ancients placed over one of their temples the inscription "Man, know thyself."

There are many things that you do not know about yourself. Some may be good and some may be bad, but there is an encouraging angle to this, namely that the good things are the enduring things and that they will outlive the bad things, because God made you good, not bad.

You cannot conceive of God as being anything less than good. Therefore you, having been made in His image and likeness, must be fundamentally good. You may not realize that you are so good, your friends and relatives may not believe it, and some of them may even think that you are otherwise. Nevertheless the spiritual pattern of God's ideal man shines through you, confirming the Truth that

49

you are perfect in Spirit. Keep this truth faithfully in mind and it will help to bring this perfection of yours into manifestation in your life. Believe in it and it will grow into expression in your life and affairs, because it is the foundation of your existence.

Because these things are true, I want to remind you, dear reader, that you are a wonderful being regardless of who you are or where you are. Perhaps you may have picked up this book by mere chance. I am writing to you also, and saying, "You are good and you are wonderful." No matter what mistakes you may have made, or what disappointing thoughts you may hold concerning yourself, or what others may have said against you, you are in Truth inherently good. Goodness is welling up in your soul seeking to find expression in your thoughts, words, and actions, and doing everything to make you radiant and happy.

You are loving and kind too. You may think that you do not like certain persons and things, even that you have enemies; but I tell you that God loves you and that the love of Christ is now ready to forgive you and to come forth in your life and make you a success. Love will help you to prove that all men and women are your brothers and sisters. It will make you happy and fearless wherever you go.

Even though you may feel that you are different from certain persons and that they do not like you or you them, it will help you to love everybody and to receive their love in return.

The real you is a loving, joyous being. You are also truthful and honest. You are dependable; you are able to spread blessings everywhere and make people happy wherever you go. Because the Spirit of God in you is the source of your life you are privileged to be well and strong. As you begin to realize that you have the power to bless and to spread happiness, the unfoldment and expression of this power will bring you great satisfaction. It will also stimulate and improve your health.

Many blessings are now ready for you, but you must invite them to come into expression in your outer life by getting acquainted with them. No longer think "I cannot do this," "I am not good," "I am not as worthy as others," "I am ill," "I am ignorant," "I am weak." All of these statements are false. They are not true of you. As a matter of fact when you begin to think about the good things that are yours by divine right, these things will begin to unfold and expand in your life.

Remember that you have an inner spiritual strength that is capable of sustaining you when you need it, no matter how great your need may be. Dependable wisdom resides in you and if you will listen to it you will always know the right thing to do. It is good wisdom because it is God wisdom.

Remember that all things are possible to you through the power of Christ in you. Within you abides your hope of glory, which means your hope of success, health, happiness, and all the good things that you would like to have and to be.

Be yourself and you will be wonderful. Do not try to be like anybody else. Do not be discouraged if the good qualities you desire to express do not shine forth in you all at once. They are already within you, but they must be encouraged to grow and develop in your outer experiences. You must not be discouraged if your growth seems slow. Make it enduring and peaceful by patience.

Remember that you are indeed a very capable, poised, and dependable person, but because you realize that it is God in you who deserves all credit for your success, you are also a humble person. As you enlarge the expression of your perfect Self, you will live more joyously, fearlessly, lovingly, and understandingly.

I have told you this secret concerning your greatness, but you do not need to keep it a secret. Pass it along to others, reminding them that they also are wonderful souls and that they may grow more wonderful in manifestation from day to day.

Those to whom you tell this secret will become more helpful both to you and themselves, because you and they will be working together in the knowledge that you are all children of the one God.

Instead of trying to be like certain notable men in the world, you will try to be like the Christ.

Too many men and women have accepted some of the lesser traits of character that they observed in others instead of unfolding their own true Godlike character.

I have called your attention to these wonderful truths about yourself, knowing that they will not cause you to become vain, because spiritual qualities cannot make you vain. When we realize that God is the true and only standard of excellence, we shall never be vain, but instead we shall grow more thankful and joyous as we learn to express unobtrusively the universal goodness that God has implanted in us.

There is therefore no need for you to become contentious, angry, afraid, or to doubt, for there is a Spirit in you that is greater than all the world. You have an unbeatable Spirit, the Spirit of the Christ of God.

"Arise, shine; for thy light is come, and the glory of Jehovah is risen upon thee."

Discouragement is a hobgoblin that men have made out of the imagination.

Those who trust in the Lord cannot be discouraged. Many persons think that they are trusting in the Lord, while all the time they are really looking for their success and happiness to come from their little personal plans. These personal plans sometimes so fill the mind that there is no room left for faith in God.

When their little personal plans fail, these people are apt to think the Lord has failed them. The fact is that they have failed the Lord.

Have you set your faith on God, or have you turned it to personal schemes? If your faith is in God and the personal scheme is a secondary consideration, you are safe, because even if the scheme should fail, you still have God.

The man who puts his faith in God may see some of his plans fail, but he will never be discouraged; he will never lose his grip, because his faith is in that which does not change. He will find a lesson and a benefit in every seeming failure, and they will help him to build better next time. No success will turn his head, but he will abide in the consciousness of the goodness of God at all times, and his personal plans will be modeled after the divine plan. He will abide in the kingdom where discouragement is unknown.

Do You Need Help?

Everybody needs help of some kind. Do not be ashamed of yourself if you feel that you need help. As a matter of fact, we all must help one another. But, also, we must remember something that is supremely important: namely, there is one helper who is the best helper of all. That helper is Jesus Christ, who has told us that He came to serve and not to be served. And He promised, "Lo, I am with you always."

How do we know that He is with us? We cannot see Him. No, we cannot see Him with our eyes, and neither can we see the life that animates us, but we know that it is in us filling us with energy, power, and intelligence.

Jesus Christ is with every one of us, but few of us are aware of His presence. In order to feel His presence and receive His help we must believe in Him and be willing to accept His help. He said: "If ye shall ask anything in my name, that will I do." When we think only of our own physical power and personal ability, we are not likely to have faith enough to call upon Jesus Christ for help. We can find Him in prayer and meditation. Faith in Him is the door that opens to us the great and perfect creative Mind of the Father.

Jesus said that it was not He Himself who did the mighty works but the Father within Him. Therefore, when we call upon Jesus Christ for help, we must know that we are calling upon the living words of God, and that when we have faith enough in Him, we shall be able to overcome the troubles of the world, not by physical force, but by the power of good according to God's plan.

God's plan includes the constructive power of

goodness, loving-kindness, forgiveness, and peace. When we ask for the help of Jesus Christ, we co-operate in employing God's good powers to overcome evil instead of employing destructive, physical powers to fight our enemies. With the help of Jesus Christ we can overcome the evils of the world with love, wisdom, and truth. Love is like light, and hate is like darkness. We cannot overcome darkness with darkness, but when we bring the light into the darkness, the darkness disappears. So it is with the light of love. It dissipates hate and fear. "Perfect love casteth out fear."

When we call upon Jesus Christ to help us, we should realize that He is very real and is as near to us as our faith in Him will permit us to accept Him to be.

When our faith is turned only toward things that we can make contact with in the outer world, we do not have enough faith left to open the door of our consciousness for Jesus Christ to come in. Jesus gave up the race ideas concerning His body so that He might lift up His body consciousness into the perfection of God's perfect-man idea, God's own image and likeness. Jesus resurrected His body consciousness into eternal life.

Jesus Christ can also help us to resurrect from the ignorant thoughts of the race consciousness our ideas concerning our body. The Adam consciousness, which has faith in both good and evil, has kept the human race in a state of mind filled with thoughts of materiality, fear, greed, unhappiness, and discord. This state of mind is not helping us to find the kingdom of God on earth. Our true goal in living is to find and express the Christ, or the perfect Son-of-God Spirit, which is within us. When we find the Christ within us, we shall not become upset by the turmoil of the world, for we shall abide in the realization of Truth and know that we are actually living in a good world that God has made. We shall then be able to help others also to find and enjoy God's perfect world.

We must have faith in Jesus Christ as a living presence within us and not think of Him as being only a historical person who lived two thousand years ago. Nor should we put Him off until a future time when He will come again into the world. The Truth is that He is with us now and, according to our faith in Him, we become conscious of His presence. He is the living shepherd within us, who leads us into paths of righteousness. When we put off His coming, we are denying Him and shutting the door of our consciousness against Him.

Christ said that He lived before Abraham was, and that He had eternal life. When we live in Him, we share eternal life with Him. We find in the 11th verse of the 8th chapter of Romans (ASV) these words: "But if the Spirit of him that raised up Jesus from the dead dwelleth in you, he that raised up

Christ Jesus from the dead shall give life also to your mortal bodies through his Spirit that dwelleth in you." Let us, therefore, seek the kingdom within us in silent prayer.

Let us continually seek the light of God and His loving harmony, which will give us victory over all things, even as Jesus Christ was victorious over all things, even death. Let us be true followers of Jesus Christ and walk with Him today, not in memories of the past nor in anticipation of the future, but today, this very moment. He is the light of the world; He is the way, the Truth, and the life. Let us walk in that way and let His light shine through us, that we may be one with the light of the world.

Jesus Christ in us is our helper, and Jesus Christ in us helps us to help others. Let us rejoice in this realization and cooperate with His divine presence and thereby really enjoy life.

Let It Pass

Holding onto an unpleasant idea is a most unprofitable way to spend your time. What if some regrettable thing did happen in the past? You cannot help matters now by keeping it in your memory. If there was a lesson in it for you, accept the lesson and resolve to do better next time.

Begin thinking constructive thoughts. Bless your past and turn it over to God's keeping. Use your present opportunity to think constructive and pleasant things, and you will make room in your life for a host of new and happy thoughts. In this way you will prepare yourself to live a more useful and happy life.

You are here on earth to enjoy life and to glorify God. Why make life drab for yourself and your associates by dwelling in the shadowy land of past mistakes? Let the past go and live now. When you release the specters of the past from your memory, they will sink away into their original nothingness.

Do the same thing with old grudges. While you hold a grudge, you are miserable. Put good will in its place, forgiving the other fellow, and you will be happy. Old grudges hurt the grudgers more than they do the "grudgee." The prayer "Forgive us our debts, as we also have forgiven our debtors" contains a formula that will cleanse your mind from festering old memories that make you sick and unhappy.

It is easy to forgive when you have first made up your mind to forgive. When you do forgive another person, you drop a mighty heavy load, for it is a fact that the heaviest burdens that men carry are in their souls.

No doubt many persons forgive their debtors only because they feel that it is their religious duty to do so, not because they want to. This seems a pity, because to forgive sincerely, with love in your heart, fills you with a powerful baptism of God's love, joy, and peace. Forgiveness is no longer a duty but a privilege.

To forgive a person who has transgressed against you actually benefits you much more than it does the transgressor. A person who will not forgive shackles himself with cold chains of his own forging. Many of life's possibilities are closed to the one who will not forgive, because he is concentrating his attention upon self instead of opening his mind to the great resources of God's love.

When you lovingly forgive someone, you open your mind to the appreciation of many new possibilities for good in your life, and you open your eyes to enjoy God's good air, sunshine, and beauty. You then understand how God is able to make His rain to fall upon the just and the unjust.

Forgiving and forgetting slights, mistakes, snubs, and all wrongs against you is the best medicine you can take to improve your health, happiness, and prosperity. You may think you are doing a favor to the person who has wronged you when you forgive him, but the Truth is that you are doing much more for yourself, because you are sweetening your life.

If you should observe that something good is being done for another person who deserves it no more than you think you do, why let it trouble you? Your own good will come to you under the divine law if you keep that law. Rejoice and give thanks always, and in that way you will be able to share in the joy of this favored person by rejoicing with him in his good fortune. If you are jealous and wonder why you were not rewarded, you only succeed in making yourself miserable. You also set up a wall of resistance about you that keeps away many blessings that God is trying to give you. When Peter, suspecting that John was to receive some favor from Jesus, asked Jesus what was to become of John, the beloved disciple, in his latter days Jesus answered: "If I will that he tarry till I come, what *is that* to thee? follow thou me."

Christ, who is within each of us, helps us to avoid envious thoughts, suggesting that we follow Him instead of our own envious imaginings. Christ leads us into an appreciation of our good, but envy, doubt, worry, and complaint concerning the good that others may receive leads us into despair and lack.

"God is no respecter of persons." When we make ourselves ready for our good, it will come to us. Let us open the way for our good to come to us by keeping our eye on the light of Truth rather than on the shadows that are cast by dark thoughts.

> Why should one who preaches God,
> By foolish zeal condemn him who
> By other means brings man to God?

Each good that's done will mingle
    with another good;
No man can keep them quite apart.
Then let us work each for one good,
And waste no time in scorn of those
Who do their good in other ways.

God Bless My Soul

There is one very near to you who needs your mercy and forgiveness. That one is yourself.

Usually when we think of being merciful, we visualize ourselves doing kind and loving deeds for other people and for dumb animals, but we need to show mercy to ourselves as well as these.

It is generally thought that men and women are more thoughtful of themselves than of others, because they are supposed to be fundamentally selfish. Perhaps this is true in a sense. We do indulge ourselves in many ways, often crowding others to one side, but at the same time we torture ourselves by self-condemnation. Of course this condemnation is generally expressed under our breath or perhaps only as a feeling of guilt or as a twinge of conscience.

Condemning a fault cannot cure it. To point out a fault may be the first step in curing it, but we cannot possibly overcome it by continuing to think of it as a reality. Something better must be put in place of the thing that is wrong to cure the fault.

If a fault in me needs curing, I can plant the seed of something better to take its place by beginning to desire to do that which is better. Then I can cultivate that desire by thinking about it and mentally dwelling upon the better thing instead of condemning the fault. I must think of what is right and stop thinking about what has been wrong. To dwell upon a past mistake is to direct my power into unprofitable channels.

If I think daily of goodness and perfection I shall be building a structure in my life that I shall not be ashamed of. Day by day I must try to measure up to this ideal as well as I can, but if I should happen to fall short, I must not condemn myself. I must learn to forgive myself and to set myself free from bondage to ideas of mistakes if I am to do better in the future. A wrong habit is somewhat like a disease. If you have a sick friend, you do not condemn him for his sickness, but you try to encourage him, and through encouragement and cheerful thoughts he thus gets well quickly.

Wrong habits of mind, heart, and hand are sick conditions that need to be cured. Encourage that weak thought in you which needs healing instead of stamping on it with a paralyzing thought of condemnation. Jesus said: "Be ye merciful, even as your Father is merciful. And judge not, and ye shall not be judged: and condemn not, and ye shall not be condemned." He does not limit this application to other people. It covers everybody and everything, including myself. If I condemn myself I shall be doing that which He advised against. Paul said: "There is therefore now no condemnation to them that are in Christ Jesus. For the law of the Spirit of life in Christ Jesus made me free from the law of sin and of death."

If we want to free ourselves from condemnation, we must put ourselves under the law of Jesus Christ, for there is no condemnation in Him. Jesus said to the woman who had sinned, "Neither do I condemn thee: go thy way; from henceforth sin no more." When we are under the law of Christ Jesus, no matter what our sins may have been we are no longer under condemnation. If we are under condemnation, it is because of our own unwise words, for Jesus also said, "by thy words thou shalt be justified, and by thy words thou shalt be condemned." Paul realized how important it was that we do not condemn ourselves when he said to the Romans, "Happy is he that judgeth not himself in that which he approveth."

Perhaps there are things you are doing that you know are not right and that other people know are not right, and you are ashamed of them and want to overcome them. Here are a few examples: Perhaps you tell a little white lie now and then to protect yourself from the opinions of others, and then afterward you are sorry and condemn yourself. Perhaps you nag your family, and then later you are sorry and condemn yourself for it. Perhaps you gossip a little and are afterward sorry and chide yourself for this breach of friendship. Perhaps you may say foolish words that you know are not productive of good; then you recall that you are held accountable for your lightest word, and then condemn yourself. Perhaps you are careless and make many mistakes because you do not pay attention to what you are doing. Perhaps you are forgetful and you condemn yourself for that. Perhaps you have bad habits of various kinds and you condemn yourself because of them. Perhaps you may have made poor investments, and you go over and over the mistakes you have made and reprove yourself for them. If you are condemning yourself for anything, stop it now and remember that condemning yourself will not cure these errors.

You need to be free from these mistakes. Condemnation keeps you in bondage. To be free you must be free from condemnation as well as free from the unprofitable habit. Since condemnation cannot free you, you must ask Jesus Christ to free you. Be willing to give up the shameful thing to Him and you will find that He will dissipate it.

If you do not succeed in becoming free the first time you try this method, keep on trying, but do not condemn yourself even if you should fall again and again. You must learn to forgive yourself seventy times seven if necessary. When you have asked Jesus Christ to forgive you, you then know that you are being forgiven indeed and that you are improving, because Christ in you cannot fail.

Keep your heart light and know that you are being made free in the consciousness of Christ's power and perfection. Realize that old, unpleasant things are passing out of your life and that you are becoming a new creature in Christ.

Friends of God

A father rejoices exceedingly when his son develops in understanding and good judgment to the degree that he becomes a companion and coworker with his dad.

When boys and girls grow up and prove they appreciate what their father has done to care for and educate them, and have grown sturdy in character by meeting wisely and fearlessly experiences in daily life, they become helpful companions and counselors in the home by aiding their father. Such children are a comfort and a blessing to their father.

How it must delight a father when he realizes that he has a child who understands him and can help solve the family problems. A son or daughter who is a true companion, with whom at the close of day he can talk over the joys and the problems of the day, glorifies such a father. In this way the father and child each contribute something constructive to the life of the home. When the son becomes a real pal to the father, he gets full measure of co-operation in return from the father.

It seems to me that our Father-God must also rejoice when one of His human children grows in spiritual understanding until he becomes a son who realizes the blessed meaning of his having been created in his Father-God's image and likeness.

When Father and son become unified in spiritual understanding, the Father will then be in a position to do His mighty works through the son. In this way the Father will be glorified in the son. When the son recognizes and has faith in his Father's power and authority, and realizes how great is His love for him, he will become a real companion to the Father.

The Almighty, our Father-God, created man with all the possibilities of perfection, but man is free to accept or refuse the blessings of the kingdom. Man is an individualized creation having free will, and not merely an automaton. Therefore when a man of his own choice consciously accepts his spiritual heritage from his Father, the Father knows that here is a worthy son who elects to be like his Father, and is therefore different from a creation that is good only because it cannot be otherwise. Here is a man who is consciously aware of his Father-God. All that the

Father has is at the disposal of the son when he steps out on faith to prove his ability to use these powers rightly.

It is not fitting that a son of God should beg and cry to his Father for the good things of the kingdom when he understands that they are his already to use wisely under divine law. When he finds his true relationship to his Father, he knows that all the Father has is gladly given him to use to the degree that his ability will permit.

God, the Father, yearns for His children to understand and love Him, and to walk with Him fearlessly. He rejoices when His sons and daughters are ready to share the responsibility of bringing His kingdom to the earth. He rejoices in the companionship of obedient sons and daughters who glorify Him by their good works. They are His loving children who take time to talk things over with Him daily, because they love to be near Him and seek His wise counsel in all their ways.

He dotes on sons who have faith enough in Him to ask His advice and guidance, and who seek His instruction before they make any new plans, in order that they may avoid the mistakes of the world, sons who accept the responsibility of becoming like Him in doing His good works, which include forgiveness, love, generosity, tolerance, order, harmony, and peace.

Jesus Christ, who was the first man to demonstrate His true sonship and consciously to unify Himself with the Father, advised His followers to become perfect also, as their heavenly Father was perfect. He realized that Father and children are all one in Truth when the children grow in understanding and accept their unity with the Father. Jesus said it this way: "That they may all be one; even as thou, Father, *art* in me, and I in thee, that they also may be in us."

A baby prince was once stolen and carried away and raised in the woods by a woodchopper. He grew up thinking that he was a woodchopper's son, thinking and acting like a woodchopper. Everyone thought that he was merely a woodchopper's son.

One day an old servant told the king where his lost son was. The king sent a messenger for the boy. As soon as the young man learned that he was a king's son, he assumed the bearing of a prince and began to think and act as a prince. He was a son of the king all the time but he had not known it.

We all are sons and daughters of a perfect Father, but we do not realize the fact.

We think that we are heirs of the flesh and that we are subject to sin, sickness, sorrow, poverty, and death. We forget that Jesus told us to call no man father, for God is our Father.

If you are sickly, stop worrying about it. Begin thinking of yourself as a child of God, who cannot be sick and who does not wish any of His children to be sick. Keep this in mind until you realize that it is an absolute fact, then you will begin to express your birthright of perfect health as a child of God. You will be a tower of strength to your friends and associates, because they will begin to see the divine in you and, seeing you as divine, they will seek the divine in themselves.

My heart is right with God.

A Prayer Drill

First Day. *I am a child of the living God. His Spirit lives in me, guiding and sustaining me. I am fundamentally good.*

Second Day. *I am willing and eager that the light of Jesus Christ shall shine out through me continuously.*

Third Day. *I am fearless, humble, forgiving, joyous, truthful, honest, loving, and wise, because these are expressions coming from the Spirit of Christ, which God has placed in my heart.*

Fourth Day. *I am dependable, true, and faithful, expressing the Christ Spirit in me.*

Fifth Day. *I am strong, courageous, and steadfast, for God is my Father.*

Sixth Day. *All things are possible with God, who dwells within me.*

Seventh Day. *The blessings of God are being poured out upon me in full measure, and I am rejoicing continually in His love.*

Chapter 3

Using Divine Substance

**Divine love through me blesses
and multiplies this money.**

The Transmutation of Riches

MATERIAL things are valuable because man wants them, and he generally wants them because he has use for them. We might say that things have value because they are thought to be useful.

As the ideals of men have changed down the ages, some things that at one time had value have lost their worth, and other things have taken their place in the esteem of men. There was a time when stone axes and arrowheads had value, and another time when spears and heavy armor were desirable. Later, large family kettles and individual millstones became useful. Now soldiers wear no armor and have no need of spears and arrows. The housewife wants a small kitchen, with no large kettles; and instead of operating a millstone she brings her meal home in little sealed packages, ready to be cooked.

We have recently added to our list of valuable things new mechanical devices that were never dreamed of in the old days. Automobiles and airships are in this class. As the ideals of the race develop along higher lines, spiritual characteristics will be appreciated more and more deeply, because they will be found useful and practical. Material things will then still have their place, but we shall cease to contend and to fight for their possession. We shall simply use them in a sensible way, and cease to value them above spiritual realities.

Striving, contending, and fighting for the possession of things consume thought energy. When a man uses up his thought energy in this manner, he has none left to use in securing heavenly riches. Everyone generates a certain amount of thought energy. We can use our own thought energy just as we please. If we choose to waste it on lesser things, we may do so.

An old fairy tale carries a good lesson along this line. Three wishes were given to someone by a fairy. These wishes had in them great possibilities, but in the story they were wasted because of the personal selfishness and ignorance of the one to whom they had been given. The wishes may represent our God-given thought power. What we need, more than anything else, is understanding, that we may use this power rightly.

The teachings of Jesus Christ point the way to the highest and most satisfactory use of this marvelous power. He said: "Lay not up for yourselves treasures upon the earth, where moth and rust consume, and where thieves break through and steal: but lay up for yourselves treasures in heaven, where neither moth nor rust doth consume, and where thieves do not break through nor steal: for where thy treasure is, there will thy heart be also." He also told us that the kingdom of heaven is within us. Since it is so near, we can be laying up these treasures now, at this present time, in our spiritual kingdom.

How shall we lay up these treasures? By transmuting material riches into spiritual riches. As I said in the beginning of this chapter, value is put upon things because of man's regard for them. Therefore things that are counted as riches are not necessarily riches in themselves, but in man's estimation they are valuable.

The love of things is a potential power. The love of things is a prophecy of the eternal riches that are in God's kingdom, and the presence of love in us shows us that we have God-given power. When we find that we have this power, then we can learn to turn it toward worthy uses. The love of things is not to be condemned, but rather lifted up so that it will be transmuted into love of the fruits of the Spirit. When we begin to love the things of the Spirit, we begin also to lay up treasures in heaven. For example, when our love for God and our fellowmen exceeds our love of money, so that we do not wrongfully treat anyone because of money matters, then we are laying up treasures in heaven. When our love for harmony and peace exceeds our desire for worldly power, so that we do not strive for position, then we are laying up treasures in heaven. When our love for righteousness exceeds our ambition to be ahead of men and applauded by men to such an extent that we are not hurt by slights, then we are laying up treasures in heaven.

Christ's teachings all point to the desirability of laying up treasures in heaven. Praying to the Father in secret rather than publicly in the marketplaces to be heard of men, going another mile with a man who has asked you to go but one, and giving love for hate—these are a few suggestions from Him. His teaching never permits any material thing to become master of the man. The Master's followers should always be greater than mere things. His followers should never be dominated or enslaved by material riches. In the account of the temptations of Jesus, when the Devil suggested that Jesus jump from a high place to show His powers, saying that it was written:

"He shall give his angels charge concerning thee: and,

"On their hands they shall bear thee up,

Lest haply thou dash thy foot against a stone," He silenced the Devil by saying: "Thou shalt not make trial of the Lord thy God." When Jesus was hungry, and the desire for material food seemed to be overmastering Him, He said to the Devil—the desire—in response to the suggestion that He turn the stones lying about Him into bread, "Man shall not live by bread alone, but by every word that proceedeth out of the mouth of God."

When a man is able to embody the God qualities in his own life, he becomes conscious of the riches of the kingdom of heaven. All things have their beginning in God.

Material things seem to be created for the purpose of feeding and meeting the various other needs of the physical body, but these things serve still another purpose; they are appliances in life's gymnasium, and we work with them in developing our spiritual powers. The overcomer wrestles with his desire for material things and, instead of going down conquered by them, rises victorious, his spiritual muscles strengthened. Job lost everything, but through that loss he gained twice as much as he had ever had before. This point of the story is a symbol of man's gaining mastery through overcoming his selfishness. "For whosoever would save his life shall lose it; but whosoever shall lose his life for my sake, the same shall save it."

Jesus did not teach that we should suffer lack or unhappiness, for He said, "Seek ye first his kingdom, and his righteousness; and all these things shall be added unto you." He said: "These things have I spoken unto you, that my joy may be in you, and *that* your joy may be made full." His teaching is for the purpose of helping everyone to lift up his love from a merely physical and mental force to a spiritual power, and thus to transmute the transitory riches of the world of appearances into the everlasting riches of the world of spiritual reality.

God's Bank

God's bank has assets so great that it is beyond man's ability to appraise them, and the best thing about it is that every man's credit is good at this bank when he complies with the rules governing withdrawals from it, for God is no respecter of persons. However, the withdrawals must be made in accordance with God's rules, for order is heaven's first law.

You have already guessed that God's bank is the kingdom of heaven. Every man can draw as large a check on God's bank as his faith will permit him to write. God's good things are like money in that they must be circulated in order to be of any help to us. Like the air we breathe, His good things must be constantly kept in circulation in order that they may benefit us. They lose their value when they are hoarded or are used selfishly.

God is the God of the living, and He is constantly

making all things new. It is God's loving desire that His children shall have in abundant measure every good thing they need. His good gifts include wisdom, health, peace, prosperity, and happiness.

Jesus Christ is the perfect incarnation in the flesh of the Son of God. Christ, incarnated perfectly in Jesus, came to prove that God wants all men also to become like Him, perfect temples of the living God. This they must do by following Jesus' teaching and example. Jesus Christ said: "I am the way, and the truth, and the life: no one cometh unto the Father, but by me." He means that we must find our unity with the Father as He did.

When we find our unity with God we can say with Jesus: "All things whatsoever the Father hath are mine." Jesus also promised: "Therefore I say unto you, All things whatsoever ye pray and ask for, believe that ye receive them, and ye shall have them. And whensoever ye stand praying, forgive, if ye have aught against any one; that your Father also who is in heaven may forgive you your trespasses." These words show us how unlimited the possibilities are for our prayers to be answered; also they point out how we ourselves limit the answer to our prayers when we are selfish and unloving.

Practicing unforgiveness is one of the selfish ways in which we often interfere with the free cashing of our prayer checks on God's bank. Jesus Christ also said: "Verily, verily I say unto you, If ye shall ask anything of the Father, he will give it you in my name. Hitherto have ye asked nothing in my name: ask, and ye shall receive, that your joy may be made full."

Here we are told what name we must sign on our check in order to draw supply from God's bank. We must use our true name to prove that we are God's son: our heavenly name, not our earthly name. We must be conscious of the Truth of our oneness with Christ in God. This consciousness brings us into the Father's house, or kingdom, where His riches abound. When we consciously reach the kingdom state of mind, our joy is made full, and we know of a Truth that in Spirit all things are ours to use as we need them unselfishly, lovingly, and generously.

Jesus also assures us: "For your Father knoweth what things ye have need of, before ye ask him." After saying these words He continued His discourse by suggesting a prayer for all of us to use. It begins: "Our Father who art in heaven." In these words Jesus refers to God as the Father of us all. What must we understand when the only-begotten Son of God asks us to join with Him in praying to "Our Father"? Does He not mean that all of us who join with Him in this prayer are God's sons also?

When we realize that in our spiritual nature we are one with Christ in God, we are admitting that we have parted with the only-begotten Son in the Father's kingdom. So when we repeat the Lord's Prayer in Spirit and in Truth we find a deeper meaning in it than we had before realized, and through this new realization we lift ourselves up into a greater degree of unity with God and Christ in Spirit. Until we realize that we are truly the only-begotten Son of God, we are like lost sheep wandering in the wilderness of material consciousness. Jesus Christ has shown us how we can become sons and sharers in our heavenly Father's riches by finding our true relationship with God in Spirit. When we do this in His name we are able to say: "I am God's son, created in His image and likeness."

In drawing a check on God's bank we must properly identify ourselves by signing it in the name of Jesus Christ. We can enter into God's kingdom and receive His riches in glory when we identify ourself as His son by doing His will. The key to the door of the kingdom is unselfish love. "Thou shalt love the Lord thy God with all thy heart, and with all thy soul, and with all thy mind." We may become joint heirs with Jesus Christ and share with Him in the kingdom abundantly if we will follow the spiritual meaning of the teaching of Jesus Christ, when He said: "If ye abide in me, and my words abide in you, ask whatsoever ye will, and it shall be done unto you."

How to Use God's Perfect Ideas

Your Father-God has given you wonderful gifts, but you will not be able to appreciate them until you seek them in spirit and in truth and then stir them up by using them.

God's gifts are His divine ideas. The universe has its foundation in ideas that are in the Mind of God. In order to bring God's ideas into manifestation in our world, we must express them. We are God's helpers, and it is our duty to find His ideas in Spirit and then to bring them into activity in our daily life.

One of God's greatest gifts to His children is His idea of love. God loves us, but in order to feel His love and to receive its full benefit, we must stir up the potential love that is within us and express it in our thoughts, words, and deeds. We can do this by giving thanks for the wonderful universe that God has prepared for us and by increasing our love for Him. We can increase our love for God until we love Him with all our mind, heart, and strength. We shall then begin to understand and find His wonderful love for us. As we stir up our gift of love for God, we shall have so much love to give that we shall joyously share it with our neighbors. Love is like a spiritual muscle, because it increases in power as it is used.

All good ideas come from God, but when we use

His ideas, we should let Him guide us in the right way to use them. An idea may come to us to do something that we have never done before; but if we allow our personal feelings to influence us, we may go about the attainment of our idea in the wrong way. Our negative emotions, such as fear, hate, jealousy, suspicion, doubt, and the like, may direct us in a narrow way wherein we may forget to include the Spirit back of the idea.

If we will ask God to direct us when we begin working out our new idea, He will show us a better way, which will help us to proceed lovingly, unselfishly, peacefully, harmoniously, courageously, and faithfully, and enable us to find joy, satisfaction, and success in the attainment of the idea.

For example, let us say that a man gets an idea for the invention of a new machine that will save time and work for many people. If he develops this new idea entirely for the purpose of making money for himself, he will not obtain the full benefit from the idea. The Spirit of God's unity is the heart of every one of His ideas, but we must work with God in Spirit if we would include the vital part of His idea in our expression of it. If the inventor will consider the machine that he is inventing as something that is for a loving service to his fellow men, and realize that this service is much more important than the monetary reward and personal glory that can come to him, he will derive greater satisfaction

than if he works for personal gain and leaves God
out of the picture. He will also find much more joy
and satisfaction in the development of his idea in
God's way, because he will feel God's love working
through him as he works to bring joy and helpfulness into the lives of others. The money he makes
and the worldly fame that comes to him should be
of secondary consideration to him, but he is bound
to prosper in an outer way.

Let us therefore accept God's good ideas and use
them in a positive, unselfish way as we cooperate
with Him according to His spiritual plan. The
whole universe expresses God's ideas in action. Our
joy of living comes from our participation in making God's ideas active in our life.

Perhaps you have a wonderful cookbook on your
shelf, filled with appetizing recipes, but you must
realize that until you use the ideas that are printed
in the recipes and put them into activity by prepar-
ing the suggested dishes, you will not know how
wonderful these ideas in the book are. When you
put your love and blessings into the dishes you prepare by following these recipes, you will add spiritual substance to them, which will bless all who
partake of them.

So it is when we use God's loving ideas: until we
practice putting our spiritual substance and love into
them, we cannot express them fully in Spirit. When
we realize that in Spirit we are one with all God's

children, we shall be able to enjoy the true power of God's harmonious, loving ideas as we work them out for the good of all our brothers and sisters.

I do not mean that we should try to force our good ideas upon anyone in an outer way. We should let our ideas of true, loving service be free to all who will accept them, but we should not try by physical or mental power to compel anyone to accept them.

God works with us to help us and to make our life happy. He does not try to compel us to accept and use His ideas, but gives us freedom to choose to do His good will or to do our own will. We are free to send our cooperative, loving thoughts and blessings to others, and we can cooperate with others in Spirit when we do not demand that they accept our ideas and do as we say. God serves us, and we, His children, should serve one another in peace, harmony, freedom, and faithfulness.

God's idea back of man is a perfect creature, as our Father is perfect in Spirit, for He created man in His own image and likeness. Therefore, we should seek to find His perfect idea, which is the Christ in us, and to believe in it so truly that we are willing to let His idea of perfection become active in our mind and body. When we do this, we shall avoid the ills that come to those who do not use God's perfect ideas or let them become active in their mind, body, and affairs.

Doctors are beginning to realize more and more that many of the ills of the flesh are caused by unhappiness and disturbance in the mind of the patient. When we work with God in Spirit and in Truth, we shall find the true joy of living and we shall share our joy with others.

The attainment of money is not in itself prosperity, for money is only a symbol of God's true prosperity. If we were wrecked on a desert island and had bags of gold, the gold would be of no value to us, because we can buy things with gold only when there are others to buy from. Therefore, let us remember that God's ideas are always at our service and know that, when we are willing to use them, we shall realize that we and all people are in Spirit children of God. Let us also remember that what we do for others we are really doing for ourselves, because we are activating God's good ideas in a harmonious and prosperous way.

Prosperity really means that we are able to appreciate and use God's spiritual ideas of abundance. These ideas include not only infinite spiritual goodness but manifest goodness, intelligence, harmony, peace, love, and substance. When we stir up the gift of God within us, we shall not need to worry about anything in the world. Our Father-God has created substance and goodness enough to supply all of His children's needs forever.

How to Stretch Your Money

Money was invented for the convenience of men in expediting the exchange among themselves of services and goods. Money should always be a servant of man and never his master.

Money was designed to help us, not to worry us. We should think of our money as a helpful friend, but not as a god to be worshiped. Money actually has no power or character of itself except that which we give to it.

Man's attitude toward his money determines whether it will be a curse or a blessing to him. If a man curses his money or curses others because he fears they are trying to get his money, then a curse will return to him. If he blesses his money and makes it a blessing to others, blessings will come home to him.

Money has no value except that which is given it by man, and its value is dependent upon a man's faith in his fellowmen. No one would be willing to accept money if he did not have faith in those who cooperate in using the money. God created the universe and all things in it. Therefore God is greater and more important than these things.

If we will remember that God is more important to us than money and things, we shall be able to maintain correct relations with our environment. When we trust in God instead of things, we shall be poised and happy. Things will never be able to control us, for we shall seek God's kingdom first, knowing that these things shall be added.

When we remember that we "live, and move, and have our being" in God, we shall not feel that we are adrift on an uncertain sea of materiality, but we shall know that we are safe in the care and keeping of our loving Father, who has created all things for our good. When we abide in this realization, we shall not be unhappy if there seems to be a temporary lack of money, for we shall know that no material thing can stand between us and God's blessings. When we go direct to God in faith and acknowledge Him in all our affairs, we shall be sustained by Him.

Money is merely a symbol of values. When we place our faith in the symbol rather than in the true value, we are disappointed. We must train ourselves to look to God directly for our prosperity and not trust too much in money.

If our income seems to be inadequate because of high prices, we must not be dismayed, but we must steadfastly realize that our good comes from God, not from money. Placing the power of God's blessing upon our money will actually make it possible for us to buy more with a given sum than we could purchase by ordinary methods.

If we realize that the money in our hand represents only a symbol of true substance, we can call out the true substance by blessing this symbol.

When we realize that there is no limit to God's substance, our faith will call God's substance into service for us and all our needs will be supplied.

Jesus understood the Truth that His good came to Him from the Father according to His faith, and He lacked for no good thing. The fish provided Him with tax money; the multitude was fed from God's invisible substance, and Jesus was always welcome to partake of food in every village He entered. He was neither a beggar nor a financier, but He had close communion with His Father, God, the Source of all good things.

It is not necessary for God to perform a miracle in order to take care of our daily needs. His wonders are performed before our very eyes through material channels when we have made contact with His substance through our faith. God will stretch anybody's income so as to cover all needs, even as He multiplied the loaves and fishes to feed the five thousand.

By blessing what we have, we increase and multiply it. We need to become attuned to the great, universal spiritual ideal back of money, which can be manifested as money or as anything else that is good. There is security in God, and we are very near to it when we go within and consult Him sincerely in spirit and in truth.

God is Spirit, and we must therefore worship Him in Spirit and in Truth. If we attempt to pray to

God for money and then while praying, because of our fears and worries, fix our attention on our need for money rather than on giving thanks to God for His abundance, we shall not be making a very successful prayer. When we give thanks for His substance and withdraw our attention from the thought of lack and place it upon God in faith and thanksgiving, we shall be heard and supplied by the Father.

Paul tells us in the 11th chapter of Hebrews that "what is seen hath not been made out of things which appear."

We know that certain invisible gaseous elements when combined will form a visible substance. For example: Hydrogen and oxygen gases combined in right proportion become visible water. But while Spirit is invisible, just as gases are, it is a much finer substance. Jesus explained Spirit to Nicodemus by likening it to the wind that blows where it pleases; man cannot see where it comes from nor where it goes.

So it is with Spirit. We cannot see it, but it is nevertheless the invisible substance out of which are formed all things that appear. An oak grows from a little acorn and expands into a mighty tree on a seemingly lean diet of water, sunshine, and microscopic amounts of chemicals in the soil. So does the mighty substance of God come forth out of Spirit and take its place in our affairs through natural channels to supply our needs.

If your present income seems to be inadequate for your needs, do not worry; do not complain; do not be critical; do not be afraid. Instead, give thanks to God for His supply and bless the symbol of substance that you have in your hand. It will grow and increase in buying power. Like the mustard seed, which grew from a tiny seed into a tree, its increase will amaze you.

God's substance is present everywhere and in Truth is more real than the things you can touch and see. Bless the good symbol you have and see substance miraculously increase in your hands.

Millions of creatures are coming into existence each day, and millions are disappearing each day, yet there is no decrease in life, for life is infinite. All qualities in Spirit are infinite. There is no beginning and there is no ending to the things of Spirit. Man can, by developing his spiritual nature, become so at one with God-Mind that he will be able to draw upon infinite supply for all his needs.

Remember that you are a child of God, and that God has provided for your use an abundance of His blessings. You can lay hold of these with your faith. "Faith is assurance of things hoped for, a conviction of things not seen." Through your faith you are able to tap the unlimited supply of Spirit. Even before you ask, all things are provided for you in Spirit. "Therefore I say unto you, All things whatsoever ye pray and ask for, believe that ye receive them, and ye shall have them."

Give thanks for the good that you desire, and have faith that it is already yours. By asking God for His blessings, you cannot possibly make anyone poorer, for the supply is unlimited in Spirit.

What Hast Thou in the House?

Every person who is in trouble, no matter how serious his need may be, has within himself something valuable, which if drawn upon in faith and prayer will help him to satisfy his needs and deliver him out of trouble.

The story told in 2 Kings about the poor widow whose two sons were about to be sold as bondsmen to pay her debts reminds us that we should not belittle our resources, no matter how meager they may seem to be.

When Elisha, the prophet, said to the weeping woman who was appealing to him for help, "What hast thou in the house?" she replied that she had nothing at all; that is to say, she had nothing valuable—only a pot of oil.

Elisha did not sympathize with her by saying: "Oh, you poor woman! I am so sorry for you because you cannot pay your debts with such meager resources."

Nor did he give her money out of his purse. Instead he gave her some very practical advice, telling her to begin to solve her problem by using that little pot of oil which she already had and increase it through her faith.

He recommended that the boys also do something to help, suggesting that they go out and borrow dishes from the neighbors, as many as they could get, and bring them home to their mother. Elisha then instructed her to take the receptacles with her into her house and, after shutting the door, begin pouring the oil that was in her little jar into the receptacles that her sons had borrowed.

She had faith, and she poured out the oil until she had filled all the vessels. And because there were no more vessels, she had to stop pouring. This increased supply of oil was then sold for enough money to pay all her debts and release her sons from possible bondage.

The supply of oil seemed to be limited only by the number of vessels that could be obtained to hold it.

It seems to me that the little pot of oil, which the widow confessed was the only possession she had left, is a symbol of a precious but little-appreciated possession that every person has within himself. When understood and rightly and prayerfully poured out, it will supply the needs of anyone who has faith and love enough to use it. It is the tiny seed idea, which through faith and prayer grows to such proportions that it can deliver a man from any kind of bondage.

I suggest that we think of our needs as opportunities to be used as receptacles into which God's increase may be poured. An empty life crying for satisfaction, if the cry is turned to God, will cause that life to become a vessel filled with the riches of God that truly satisfy. The empty vessels borrowed from neighbors may represent to us opportunities for pouring out our blessings and good thoughts upon others. By pouring them out thus we can increase our ability to draw more heavily upon the infinite Resource.

Oil represents joy and praise, which make life run smoothly. Even if we are without material food, we still have that oil of Spirit within us which we can pour out to fill up the empty places in our life and the lives of our friends. We may wonder what good the increase of the spirit of joy and praise can do in supplying our material needs. In the story, the widow sold the increased supply of oil and then paid her debts with the money she received for it.

Joy and praise are worth money, because they are what all the world is seeking. Like other spiritual gifts, these are enjoyed and increased most when they are given away or shared. Giving and sharing God's gifts brings more joy to the giver than receiving and hoarding can bring to the receiver.

Those who depend upon the possession of many things to bring them happiness and satisfaction will remain hungry in soul even though their barns may be bursting, because material things alone cannot fill the emptiness of the inner man. It is the pouring out of the riches of Spirit in prayer that satisfies both the soul and the body.

When we give or express life we increase our capacity for living. When we express wisdom, we grow wiser. When we love, we increase our consciousness of love. When we are joyous, we increase our joy. When we exercise our strength, we grow stronger. Our labors and our experiences in the material world should help us increase our inner, spiritual resources. These include life, love, wisdom, strength, and other attributes of the spiritual man. These grow and expand by proper use, which proper use is the pouring-out process.

Spiritual riches have been given to every man and woman by our Father-God, abundantly; and as we prayerfully pour out these gifts, even though at first they may seem to be small, they will surely become great through faith and works. Their possible greatness will be limited only by the capacity of the vessels that we have provided to hold them.

We can discover the limitless nature of the blessings that God has given us when we draw freely upon them by pouring them out. We can pour them out with such faith and love that we shall inspire others with the desire to pass their blessings along also.

The gifts of God are limited only by a person's capacity to express them or pour them out. We can supply our needs for outer things by first drawing the oil of Spirit from within. This in turn will bring the money to buy what we need. The one who learns how to pour out this inner substance which God has given him will lack for no good thing in the world.

Let no one despair because he may seem to have little to draw upon. Rather let him look within and rejoice in the abundance that God has given him in Spirit, and then let him fearlessly give forth what he finds in the house.

The Secret of Giving

God has given His children all things, and each child can have as much as he is able to receive and use. We, His children, are here on earth to demonstrate our divine sonship by using wisely and unselfishly the rich gifts of our Father-God. He gives to us freely according to our ability to understand our responsibility in using His gifts properly.

When we begin to realize and to appreciate spiritually the wonders of God's creation, we are like an explorer visiting a new country filled with beautiful and amazing opportunities. We discover beautiful, interesting, and wonderful things everywhere.

Since God has given us everything, potentially, we must learn how to discover His gifts by making them spiritually active in our life. We can do this by passing them along to others with our love and blessings. Divine ideas become real to us and active in us when we share them with others.

The air we breathe is most necessary to keep us alive, but we must constantly breathe it out so that we can breathe fresh air back into our lungs. God has given us His love, which we must keep in action by breathing it out to other persons and to God to make room in our heart for a new supply of love.

We must share God's spiritual gifts before they can increase and become real in our lives. For example, when knowledge is shared, it increases for all concerned. Good will increases when it is shared.

When we share with others our substance and our blessings, they increase for us and for others as the loaves and fishes increased for Jesus and the multitude. When we share garden seed with God by sowing it in the ground, it increases. We cannot increase any good thing that God has given us by hoarding it. God's good gifts must be kept active in our lives to be helpful to us. When we speak kind words, kindness is multiplied in our life. When we praise God and give thanks to Him for the good things He has provided for us, our thanksgiving and praise circulate between God and us as joy, health, and prosperity.

When we give a material thing out of necessity or because we feel obligated to give it, we do not truly give in the true Christ Spirit, because we do not share the spirit of God's good substance. A true gift should bear with it our blessings and good will and our love. As the poet has said:

> "He gives only the worthless gold
> Who gives from a sense of duty."

To give truly we must put our heart into our gift. As the poet has also said:

> "The gift without the giver is bare;
> Who gives himself with his alms
>   feeds three,
> Himself, his hungering neighbor,
>   and me."

Jesus said: "Give, and it shall be given unto you; good measure, pressed down, shaken together, running over, shall they give into your bosom. For with what measure ye mete it shall be measured to you again." He also charged His disciples when sending them forth on their mission to preach the gospel: "Freely ye received, freely give."

God has given us so freely of His strength, power, love, life, joy, wisdom, peace, and harmony that we must become His active agents to express these gifts in our life. When we do, we become thrilled with the power of their goodness. When we give anything truly, we help to satisfy a spiritual hunger in our own heart as well as in the heart of the ones to whom we give. We also strengthen our spiritual contact with the heart of God where all good things originate.

Forgiveness is also a kind of giving, but it acts more as a soul cleanser than as an activator, for it erases the errors of the past from our mind. When we forgive a fault we give up, or cast out of our memory, negative experiences, and they become as nothing to us. When these things are forgiven and forgotten, they henceforth have no place in us. Such things are not increased by giving, but are decreased by forgiving.

The success of our life is determined by what we think, say, and do. By sharing our good with others and with God in our thoughts, words, and deeds, we increase the power and activity of good in our life and affairs.

Tithing is one way of working with God's substance and increasing it by sharing it in Spirit in helping to take care of the Father's business. God does not need our substance, but we need His cooperation, and we need to prove the unfailing quality of

His substance by joyously sharing it in the spirit of faith and love.

The currency of our country would be of no value if it were not kept in circulation. It represents the substance of God, which is most valuable when it is kept in circulation. And as we do our part in circulating God's substance in Spirit and in Truth, we increase not only our own prosperity but the prosperity of our community.

We bring more substance and goodness into realization in our own life, as well as glorify God, when we share our good substance in the name of God's abundant supply. Therefore let us join God in the joyous game of giving and receiving. Let us prove to our Father-God that we have received His bounty by giving bountifully in Spirit and in Truth. I am not thinking merely of money, but of divine substance, which sustains not only money and worldly riches, but also sustains our whole being. We live more richly when we keep the good things of our life moving by using and sharing them for God's glory.

Ask for More

Remember that the divine supply is greater than the human demand.

Man asks too meagerly, calling for inferior things when he might just as easily call for the best. The average person prays as if he felt that he might be robbing someone else if he asked for enough to supply all his needs, or as if the supply in the divine storehouse were running low.

I heard recently of a man who prayed that he might get to his mother's bedside before she died, and his prayer was answered. He could, however, just as well have prayed that his mother be healed. Another man prayed that his brother be allowed to die without pain. The God of Jesus would have healed his brother.

On a cold, snowy day a tired woman with a big bundle of groceries in her arms prayed that she might ride at least part of the way home. Sure enough, when she had gone two-thirds of the way, a friendly neighbor picked her up in his automobile and took her the remaining one-third of the way. She could have asked to be taken all the way home.

When I was a boy, I was impressed with the philosophy of an old doctor, a friend of our family. He said that he had prayed all his life for just enough to supply his daily needs, but had not asked for a bit more, and he said his prayer had been answered; he had never lacked for anything in his life, but he had had no luxuries. He was content, but God would have given him more if he had asked for more.

If you were hungry, you could just as well ask for a square meal as for a crust of bread. Remember that the divine invitation is "Ask, and ye shall receive."

Jesus Christ said: "Hitherto have ye asked nothing in my name: ask, and ye shall receive, that your joy may be made full." He also promised: "And whatsoever ye shall ask in my name, that will I do, that the Father may be glorified in the Son. If ye shall ask anything in my name, that will I do."

When we ask for a pittance, we usually do so because we feel that there is not enough for all. This feeling shows that our faith in God's inexhaustible abundance is weak. All things in nature have been provided lavishly. More seed is produced by plants than the soil can accommodate. Compared with the universe of stars and space, our earth is so small that it is hardly a speck of dust, and compared with the size of the earth, our personal needs are infinitesimal.

Surely the few extra grains of microscopic supply that we might ask for would make no difference to an infinite God who controls the vast universe. In what way then is man's supply limited if it is not limited by God's will? The limitation is in man's own capacity to receive. The very fact that he cannot ask largely proves that his capacity is limited.

Man's capacity is limited largely by the fact that he lacks a sense of spiritual values. He thinks material things are more important than spiritual things. The power to use and enjoy material things depends upon a better understanding of spiritual things. The things of Spirit are far more valuable than the things of the physical world.

If you were to pray: "God, give me a million dollars," you probably would not get it because you would not have faith that you would get it, and you would not have the ability to use it wisely. It would be much wiser to pray for wisdom, love, and understanding enough to be able to appreciate a million dollars. We need to pray for a greater capacity to live and understand life. God has already given us more than we are using. We must learn to use what we have.

God does not withhold His blessings just to hear us pray and cry for them. He has already given us all things, and He desires that we enjoy them. Our prayers should be said for the purpose of opening our own consciousness so that we may be able to see, understand, and use the omnipresent good that God has given us. Jesus said: "Yet seek ye his kingdom, and these things shall be added unto you." Instead of praying for a large sum of money in order to bring you happiness, why not pray for happiness in the first place?

We should never make the mistake of praying for something that belongs to another person or that will interfere with another's liberty. To pray that John will do this or that is not a large prayer nor a fair prayer. It is a little, narrow, selfish prayer. But to pray that John be freed to do the will of the Father takes all condemnation and limitation from him, leaving him free to do the will of his highest nature.

This is a big prayer because it asks that John's highest good be fulfilled, not just our own idea about his good.

If you want a vacation, pray for a vacation but do not limit your vacation by interfering with other persons' rights and wishes. Do not stipulate that father, mother, or sister must go with you. Pray for the vacation that you have in mind or something better.

Make your prayers definite, but do not make them inflexible. Always be ready to receive something better than the particular thing you have prayed for, and always remember that happiness, health, love, wisdom, harmony, and peace are much more to be desired than material things. In fact, when you have found the spiritual blessings, you will have entered the kingdom of God in your earthly experience, and the other things, the material supplies, will be added.

When you pray, do not assume the role of a beggar but of a master. Go to God unhampered by fear, worry, suspicion, or doubt. Do not question in your heart God's ability, but rather give thanks that He is now answering your prayers. Ask largely. Give your whole self to God, and accept His riches freely.

God is your loving Father. Do not allow your selfish personal reservations to hold back your spiritual impulses, and God will not hold back anything from you.

**Divine love through me blesses
and multiplies this money.**

A Prayer Drill

First Day. *As I bless, consecrate, and rightly use the little things that I find in my possession, they grow, and I begin to discover how great is God's loving, generous supply for me.*

Second Day. *The oil of God's bountiful supply is sufficient to fill all the empty places in my soul, body, and affairs.*

Third Day. *The source of my security abides within me, where dwells the Spirit of God, my Father.*

Fourth Day. *By exercising my faith in God's all-sufficient supply, I am able to draw upon it for all my needs.*

Fifth Day. *Putting my God-given talent to work for Him brings me joy and success.*

Sixth Day. *The riches of God's creative word are the source of all supply.*

Seventh Day. *I am thankful that my Father-God supplies me richly as I make myself ready to use that greater supply wisely and well.*

Chapter 4

The Magnetism of Love

I am a radiant center of divine love.

Awake!

YOU can cram book information into your head, but you cannot cram abilities into yourself, for God has already placed them in you. You must find them and bring them out in your life by cultivating them. True education means to draw out the abilities that are within you. They are gifts that God has placed within you for you to find and develop.

God is wisdom, love, life, power, harmony, substance, and goodness. Man, who is created in God's image and after His likeness, therefore must also embody wisdom, love, life, power, harmony, substance, and goodness.

Few men or women have even scratched the surface in discovering the wonderful potential abilities that are sleeping within them. Jesus Christ came in human form to show us how to discover and use our God-given abilities in our present environment.

He taught how each person can find his loving Father, God, by going to Him in Spirit and in Truth.

Man has tried to learn about and to unfold his mental and physical abilities, leaving his spiritual abilities mostly undeveloped. Jesus tried to show all men how to find and use their spiritual abilities in their daily affairs as well as in their devotional periods. While Jesus' teachings concern spiritual principles, His words are nevertheless very practical for use in our daily dealings with other persons.

The Spirit in man, when it is given the opportunity, will control and harmonize all his outer actions. Every person in the whole world has spiritual abilities placed within him by the Father, which are like the Father's, but the human race as a whole is making very feeble efforts to cultivate them.

If we would attain the true stature of a child of God, we must begin at once to awaken our spiritual nature, which is like God's, and develop it by practicing its principles in our daily life. In his message to the Ephesians, Paul said: "Wherefore *he* saith, Awake, thou that sleepest . . . and Christ shall shine upon thee."

Christ is the perfect spiritual Son of God, created in the image and likeness of God. This Christ is the light, which is potentially in every man. When we wake up our Christ nature, we begin to see the light of Truth. To be awake means that our spiritual eyes are open to the character of the Christ in us.

Everyone has within him many abilities and possibilities, both physical and spiritual, of which he is not yet aware because he has not awakened to their presence in him. Birds have an ability within them that tells them how to build their own kind of nest and when to migrate. These abilities in birds do not come from without, nor from the bird mother's teaching, because sometimes the baby bird never sees its mother. The ability comes from something God-given that dwells within the bird.

We human beings have such inner abilities that cause us to eat and to move about, to see, and to make noises in our throat, which noises gradually develop into speech. But these are only a part of our fund of abilities. Our human abilities are developed largely through our contact with the material realm, while our spiritual abilities must be developed by contact with the spiritual realm within us and by our application of its principles in our life and affairs.

The average man lives mostly in the material realm and devotes his attention to it instead of to the spiritual realm within himself. He has not awakened to an awareness of the greater possibilities that lie dormant within him.

Isaiah said: "Awake and sing, ye that dwell in the dust."

Love is one of the most important spiritual qualities, and it is only partially expressed in the average
individual. The deeper love of Spirit is the fulfill-
ment of all law, and when it is expressed by a person
in his thought, word, and actions, it brings unity
and harmony to his mind and body, and to all persons with whom he comes in contact. Writing to
the Romans about the law of love, Paul said, "And
this, knowing the season, that already it is time for
you to awake out of sleep; for now is salvation
nearer to us than we *first* believed."

As we study and meditate upon the spiritual
principles of love, peace, harmony, and good will,
which Jesus explained, we begin to be more alert to
understand the meaning of our spiritual inheritance
from God. Paul said: "Be ye therefore imitators of
God, as beloved children." In order to imitate God
we must develop our God qualities, which He has
given us. Jesus realized how necessary it is for all
men to awake from the deep, deathlike sleep of
mortal consciousness. Before He healed the child
who was apparently dead, He said to those who
were weeping in the house, "Weep not; for she is
not dead, but sleepeth." Then He took her hand
and raised her up, and she lived.

Jesus also spoke of Lazarus as having fallen
asleep. When He was told that Lazarus was dead,
He replied, "Our friend Lazarus is fallen asleep;
but I go, that I may awake him out of sleep." Christ

will awaken us from our sleep in sense consciousness when we ask Him with faith to do so.

It is interesting to note the symbolism that is
shown in the story of Jacob, who was on his way to
his uncle's home in the far country of Haran. One
night he fell asleep with only a stone for a pillow. In
the morning he woke up with a new idea, a vision of
God. "And Jacob awaked out of his sleep, and he
said, Surely Jehovah is in this place; and I knew it
not."

We are all pretty much like Jacob. We think that
conditions are hard and unproductive, but when
we wake up to the truth that God is with us always,
we say: "Surely God is in this place, and I knew it
not."

When we are in trouble and feel that everything
is going wrong, if we will open our spiritual eyes
and become awake to spiritual reality, we shall see
that God is actually here in this very unlikely environment, and we did not know it. This story of
Jacob is in accord with Jesus' statement, "The kingdom of God is within you."

Wherever we are, the kingdom of heaven is with
us, but when we are spiritually asleep we are
unaware of it. We may think that the kingdom of
this world is the only kingdom touching our life,
and if we think this way, we shall continue to be at
the mercy of outer circumstances. But when we call
out the spiritual power of Christ within us, and use

it, we shall demonstrate dominion over our circumstances.

Let us look first within ourselves and find the Christ light. Christ will reveal the Father to us and we shall become awake to and discover the Father's gifts in us. These are the spiritual faculties of truth, faith, strength, judgment, love, power, imagination, understanding, will, order, zeal, renunciation, and life.

We can do all things through Christ, who strengthens us. We must never say, "I am not able," for such an attitude belittles the inheritance that God has given us. Finding our spiritual abilities and bringing them out into expression glorifies God instead of our own selves.

If our desire is to develop our physical and mental abilities simply to glorify our personal ego, life will disappoint us. Egotism closes the channel through which God's greater power flows to us. Therefore let us do all things to the glory of God, and rejoice in His power, wisdom, and glory working in and through us.

We should never be afraid that we shall not receive credit or praise for our good works, for God has given us all things. His glory in us is a greater reward than the praise of men.

Try This Experiment

Remember that "the proof of the pudding is the eating."

Here is a taste of metaphysical pudding that I suggest you sample. If you like it, maybe you will want it for a steady diet.

This food is designed to feed the inner, or spiritual, man. This man in us must be fed, you know, and when he is well fed, all is well with the physical man. We are surrounded at all times by a bountiful feast of spiritual food that has been prepared by our loving Father, but we just do not seem to know how to get up to the table and help ourselves.

One of the most essential nourishing items on God's table is infinite love. Many of us think of infinite love as something so far above us that we cannot possibly appropriate it as we do food and use it for our daily needs. As a matter of fact, God's love is closer to every one of us than we realize. It is so close that we need only think about it earnestly to discern that it is already in our heart. Therefore we need often to remind ourselves of the reality and immanence of God's love.

For this purpose I am suggesting a simple Truth statement for you to use. I think it will help you to become aware of the presence of divine love in a more definite way. Here is the statement:

"Divine love is now working through me to adjust all the details of my life."

This is a short statement and easy to memorize. If it does not appeal to you at first, try it out anyway just for fun. Sit quietly and think about the wonderful possibilities of divine love. Write the statement down in your own handwriting and put it somewhere in your room where you can look at it occasionally. Then carry it in memory with you during the day, and when you have a few moments to spare, repeat it and think about its meaning. This will help you to get in step with the rhythm of God's love.

As you say it over, just imagine that the great healing, prospering love of the Father is infolding you and protecting you from all harm. Realize that not only is divine love infolding you and protecting you but that it is bubbling up within you and flowing forth from you in loving, friendly thoughts and emotions to all the people that you meet and to others at a distance that you know about but do not see.

Divine love is not a static force. It is dynamic, and it will set you athrill with its power. *"Divine love is now working through me to adjust all the details of my life."* Repeat this statement until it becomes a living, moving force in you and in your affairs.

Do not think of it as a charm or as something whose efficacy depends upon many repetitions, but repeat it with the conviction that you are stating a spiritual Truth. Concentrate your thought upon the meaning of it, and as you do so the literal words will seem to open and unfold before your inner eye, and your understanding of the magnitude of God's love in you will increase and amaze you.

When thoughts of divine love begin moving in your mind, their effect will be seen in your affairs, creating greater harmony and order in your relations with others.

As you develop the spirit of harmony and love within yourself, others will unconsciously be affected and harmonized. Conditions will also seem to become more friendly and thoughts of worry and fear will drop away from you, because you will be so secure in the consciousness of God's love that you will not be disturbed by outer conditions. You will understand how David felt when he sang:

> "I will fear no evil;
>   for thou art with me;
>   Thy rod and thy staff,
>   they comfort me."

The trial Truth statement is meant to be a reminder to you of God's love, which has always been and always will be with you. By repeating the statement and thinking of it as a living Truth, you will become more and more conscious of God's love as an ever-present reality.

By dwelling upon this idea, you will be able to

quicken within you a warmth of divine love that will transform your life. Your affairs will move more smoothly than ever before, for love is a lubricant like oil and will make life's machinery run more easily.

Keep your mind fixed upon the thought that God is of more importance than any earthly thing. That is, when you are meditating, do not think about the conditions that need to be improved, but fix your attention upon the perfect conditions in God's kingdom. In this way you will hold the reality of the true conditions before your mental vision. It is faith in this reality that really counts for a harmonious, happy life. First must come the vision of the Truth, and then it will work out in your affairs according to law, naturally.

Why not take time to make a thorough test of this little experiment and prove the goodness of this divine pudding? Give it a fair trial, and I am sure you will find that it will open the way for many blessings to come into your life. Here then we have given a definite, simple idea that anyone can work on.

All blessings have their source in Divine Mind. Go direct to Divine Mind and tap its resources. This will not be a difficult undertaking but a very simple one. We enter the kingdom of God by becoming as little children. Therefore with childlike faith and simplicity let us enter the kingdom of God's love.

This statement is not the only way to find divine love, but since you must have something definite to use in bringing your mind into contact with the divine source of love, the statement may help you to find God's love in your own heart.

Freedom

No person can attain his highest possible state of development—physical, mental, and spiritual—until he uses his God-given powers freely. Things that seem to be obstructions to our spiritual progress may arise in the pathway of our outer affairs, but these, in many cases, are due to our own wrong thinking. But when we are innocent of wrong thinking and obstructions do actually originate in some outer circumstance or from some other person's ignorance or malice, we must not give up to them and feel sorry for ourself. We must remember that we are free so long as we do not permit our spirit to be bound or beaten by our acceptance of the possibility that these negative conditions can have any power over us. So long as we keep our faith in God free, we shall be free.

Freedom means "liberation, choice of action, ease, facility, spiritual self-fulfillment, and absence of restraint or repression." The free individual is one who is not in bondage spiritually, mentally, or physically to any person, habit, law, or mental attitude.

The person who would be truly free must not permit himself to interfere with the freedom of any other person. He must not even hold a loved one such as a member of his family in bondage to his own personal wishes and plans. He must work according to God's law by helping his loved one to accept of his own free will the guidance and freedom of God's wisdom. He can help guide and train his child, but in doing so he should not allow his personality to dominate the child's.

The spiritual principles that underlie the physical manifestation of man in this world are all friendly to him. Because his life depends upon these spiritual principles, man is freest when his thoughts and actions are most nearly in accord with them. Even though these principles cannot change themselves to suit the whims of a person, they are not cruel or vengeful. They were not formulated to enslave man but to insure his well-being so that he may live and grow to be more like his Maker. They are like a smooth highway that has been constructed for the convenience of motorists. The highway serves those motorists best who use it rightly and observe its traffic regulations.

Often unwise laws are made by men who are selfish or who do not have the vision to understand the needs of a situation. These laws may take away some freedom from certain of the people, but after all, man-made laws are seldom perfect, and they cannot always bring justice to every man under every circumstance. Nevertheless these man-made laws are necessary at our present stage of progress. Most of these are fair and helpful because they supplement the divine laws.

By observing and complying with God's laws, any person may become free. In order to work freely and do his best work a man's hands must not be bound, his eyes must not be covered, and his Spirit must not be trammeled by fear, doubt, or greed. Free use of hands and eyes and spiritual powers was planned for man by his loving Father so that he might cooperate with Christ in doing the Father's business. But a man can hardly be free who thinks, speaks, and acts in ways that are contrary to the laws underlying his very being.

Every man should declare his freedom from selfishness so that he may do the will of his Maker and become perfect, free, happy, healthy, and prosperous. As a man comes closer to the law of his spiritual being, he becomes freer.

Every person in every land should be free to think, speak, and worship as he chooses so long as he does not use this freedom to interfere with the freedom of other persons. When laws are made by men that place other men in bondage to them, such lawmakers and the ones who enforce the laws are thereby binding themselves. They place themselves in a situation somewhat like the officer who handcuffs himself to his prisoner. Both are bound by the same chains.

I cannot be free when I am a bond servant to fear, malice, willfulness, greed, jealousy, sadness, lust, or unforgiveness. God has given all His children potential freedom to live and enjoy the wonders of His universe. All things are here for our use and pleasure, and when we comply with the guidance of the Spirit of Truth and realize that love is the fulfilling of the law, we enjoy health, peace, joy, prosperity, poise, and harmony.

In order that a wheel may run smoothly, it must turn freely on its axle. In order that a man's life may run smoothly, it must turn freely on God's good principles. We know that one of God's most important principles is love. When a person is loving and kind and lives according to the Golden Rule, his life runs smoothly; but when he is unloving, unforgiving, and hateful, he is continually running into rough experiences. We cannot be free when we are bond servants to hate and unforgiveness.

Freedom is so definitely a part of God's desire for man that the urge for freedom often asserts itself like an explosion in human affairs when the pressure of bondage becomes too strong to bear. Such explosions may take the form of social, religious, or political reforms, or perhaps in a declaration of independence, or, in the words of Truth students, in a declaration of Truth.

When the bondage of slavery became too unbearable to the Children of Israel, Moses arose and led them out of Egypt.

Jesus declared to those who were bound by sin, sorrow, and sickness: "Ye shall know the truth, and the truth shall make you free."

When we find ourselves in bondage to ideas of sickness, depression, unhappiness, fear, or worry, then it is time for us to free ourselves by declaring the Truth about our freedom in Christ. Paul said: "There is therefore now no condemnation to them that are in Christ Jesus. For the law of the Spirit of life in Christ Jesus made me free from the law of sin and of death."

God's law for man is eternal life. Death came by Adam's willfulness, and eternal life must come by Christ's righteousness. Death came by sin. Sin means missing the mark of divine perfection. It is not the Father's fault if man will not obey the law of his being. However someday God's patience with man will be rewarded by man's measuring up to the Christ standard of life.

Since it is the Truth that sets us free, we should find out what the Truth is. Jesus said, "I am the way, and the truth, and the life." He also said, "I will pray the Father, and he shall give you another Comforter, that he may be with you for ever, *even* the Spirit of truth: whom the world cannot receive; for it beholdeth him not, neither knoweth him: ye know him; for he abideth with you, and shall be in you." Here we have the key to unlock the door to our freedom. This key is the Spirit of Truth, the Christ, which is within each one of us.

We must search for the Spirit of Truth within ourselves and help others to find this Spirit in themselves so that they may also be free to accept the leading of the Spirit of Truth in their own way. When we no longer try to bind other persons, we find that we are unbound. When we are free from our own willfulness, then the outer conditions about us begin to loosen their grip on us. All conditions in our life that bind us have their beginning in the mind of man, and that man is quite likely to be ourself.

God Needs You

God's spirit works through all men, but it works most effectively in the man who believes in the goodness of God's creation.

God is the very life in our body; but unless we consciously join Him in singleness of purpose by accepting our life from Him and glorifying it as holy, good, and perfect, we shall not enjoy life abundantly. Everything we have, including the air we breathe, the sunshine that gives us heat and light, and the earth under our feet, comes from God; but when we see evil in these good things, we fail to see God's creation as He sees it. We are beholding two worlds—a good one and an evil one. God created only one world, and it is good.

Jesus said: "If therefore thine eye be single, thy whole body shall be full of light." He also said: "It is your Father's good pleasure to give you the kingdom." The kingdom is the perfect creation in which God's goodness, harmony, and beauty are realized by man. When a man accepts this perfect state of goodness, he enters into the kingdom of heaven.

God created all things perfect and good in His world. His world is the spiritual reality underlying and sustaining the manifest world. God in His love made man in His own image and likeness to become a companion and helper to Him. This man is the perfect Christ man who was created in the beginning. Christ is the true Spirit of God's ideal man dwelling in every man.

God's intention, it seems to me, was to create a physical being who would be able to help Him bring His spiritual world into manifestation on the physical plane. The allegory of the Garden of Eden shows how Jehovah God, or the Christ man, gave Adam, the first manifest man, the Garden to care for. This Garden was beautiful and perfect in every respect, and Adam was appointed to dress it and keep it. But since God's perfect love also includes freedom, His beloved son was accorded freedom to think and act as he would. If he were not free to think and act in his own way, he would be merely an automaton, who would not be able to love his Father as his Father loves him.

God made to grow in the Garden a tree that was known as "the tree of the knowledge of good and evil." This tree was not an evil tree, but it represents the negative results of freedom unwisely used. God's infinite love permits His children to exercise freedom of choice. If they elect to see evil, they are permitted to do so, and they learn a lesson from their mistake.

When man keeps his eye single to the good, he does not eat the fruit of the tree of the knowledge of good and evil. Jehovah God instructed Adam not to eat the fruit of the tree, but He permitted him access to it. When Adam exercised his freedom to disobey God's instructions, he created in his own mind belief in two powers—one good, and the other evil—thereby setting up in his mind, a false god who tormented him. Thus Adam put himself out of the good Garden by his own acceptance of the idea of two powers.

Temptations come to all of God's free children, and many are putting themselves out of the good Garden as they set up the god of evil in their midst. Jesus Christ points the way for men to overcome the god of evil by loving the true God with all their mind and strength. In this way Satan can be overcome, for he lives only in the thoughts of men. Even

Jesus, when Satan tempted Him in the wilderness, met this same problem that had confronted Adam and Eve; but He did not permit it to overcome Him. He maintained His faith in God's perfection and goodness as He kept His eye single to the truth that there is only one God, and He is good. Jesus' body was filled with life so vital that it overcame the last enemy—death—after He was crucified. Once when a suffering woman touched His garment while He was surrounded by a crowd, she was healed by her own faith. This is an example of how God's law works through the person who believes in His good power to heal.

Through faith we are able to see the reality of God's perfection in our body. When we allow ourselves to believe in the reality of conditions that appear to be evil, we are overcome by them. Through the ages man is educating himself to see only God's perfect creation in his own body and in the world about him. When he ceases to eat of the fruit of the tree of the knowledge of good and evil, he will be able to eat of the tree of life as Jesus did. When he is able through his eye of faith to see that God is everywhere present, he will become a perfect co-worker with God, and will enjoy the glory that he had with God in the beginning.

God longs for the companionship of every man. He sends His Spirit in the image of His perfect Son to carry His light to all men, and those who have had their fill of darkness in their lives will begin to seek the good things that God has prepared for them.

The things in the material world are not evil, but man's lack of understanding of God in them makes some of them seem evil to him. When things seem to go wrong, remember that all things made by the loving God are good. It is our privilege to work with God through our faith and love by seeing His goodness everywhere. In this way we can help others also to understand that God's will is good, and that they are living in it. We can help them through our faith to become conscious of this unity with God.

Freedom is a part of divine love. Jesus said that the Father makes His rain to fall upon the just and the unjust. Surely this shows the great freedom He gives as a part of His love for His children. When we can send out our love to both the just and the unjust, we shall surely be getting closer to an understanding and expression of God's great love and goodness.

You Asked for It

In his Sermon on the Mount, Jesus states a universal law in these words: "Ask, and it shall be given you; seek, and ye shall find; knock, and it shall be opened unto you: for every one that asketh receiveth; and he that seeketh findeth; and to him that knocketh it shall be opened." This is the law of asking and receiving.

We are all asking for something every day, even though we may not put our request into words. When we ask selfishly, we usually ask unwisely and as a result we receive things that we may eventually wish we had not received. We should therefore learn to be wise in our asking. This we can do by asking for understanding first so that we shall know how to ask only for those things which will be good for us and all persons concerned. We will not then ask for something that belongs to another person.

When we ask for good things, we receive good things. We often ask for things by fixing our attention upon them. Jesus Christ promised: "Whatsoever thou shalt ask of God, God will give thee it." Therefore we should fix our attention upon God and His good things instead of fixing our attention upon the things of the world that we think we want more than we want God.

Many times we fix our attention upon trouble by hating some person or thing. When we do, we make a request for trouble, and eventually we receive the trouble we asked for.

It is a good idea to ask God to give us wisdom before we ask for other things. Then we shall be directed how to ask aright. We must be wise in asking, for if we ask foolishly, we may receive what we do not really want.

As surely as we go in the direction in which we are looking, we find what we are seeking. When we seek God with our whole heart, we shall receive His good things and we shall also find Him in all the people we meet; but when we seek our own selfish desires with our whole heart, we meet selfishness in other people.

We often hear it said that someone was looking for trouble and he found it. Looking for trouble is a way of asking for trouble. Looking for harmony and goodness in other persons is one way of asking for harmony and goodness. When we follow the Golden Rule by doing for others the good things that we should like to have them do for us, we are asking for their loving cooperation. When we act toward others as we should like to have them act toward us, in a loving way, we are asking the Christ in them for His love and cooperation.

It is interesting to note how we find what we are interested in even when we search in unlikely places for it. When I was a boy, the man who lived next door was deeply interested in Indian relics. He therefore collected a large number of them, including several thousand arrowheads and other stone implements. When he walked in a field or by a roadside, he was always looking for arrowheads, and he found them. I have strolled with him in the woods and by the roadside, and have seen him pick up arrowheads in unexpected places. He interested me to the extent that I began looking for arrowheads, too, and I found several in places close to our home where I had never suspected they would be. This example shows that it is possible to find things we are looking for right where we are.

This being true, how necessary it is for us to look only for the things that are good and that we really want. When we go into the garden to pick fruit, we look for good fruit and pick that only. We do not fill our baskets with spoiled or unripe fruit. As he passes along a street, an architect finds interesting buildings and dwellings, while a gardener traveling the same street looks for and finds interesting growing plants and shrubs. Each finds the things he is interested in.

When we are looking for the Christ in the hearts of the people we meet, we find Christ; but when we are looking for faults and shortcomings in the people we meet, we find them.

"Seek, and ye shall find." That is the law, so let us be very careful to seek for worthy things, and when we seek God with our whole heart, we shall find Him everywhere. Because He is the source of all good things, He opens the windows of heaven and supplies all our needs when we seek Him. This is another way of saying: "Seek ye first his kingdom, and his righteousness; and all these things shall be added unto you."

Let us therefore stop looking for mistakes, troubles,

and evil, because to do so means that we are asking for these things. Let us look for good everywhere and thus ask for good.

Even though many other people are seeking for negative things, and such things are sometimes considered to be the most interesting items of news, let us join the great and growing number of people who are searching for news concerning goodness manifesting itself in the lives of men. By so doing we shall be helping to bring the kingdom of heaven to the earth, for the promise is that where two or three are gathered together in the name of the Christ, what they ask shall be done for them. That which we ask for in the name of Christ is always good, loving, peaceful, joyful, and satisfying.

Laugh and Relax

Man is the only creature on earth that truly laughs. Also, man is the only creature that has power to use his brain to reason and to plan things that he can make with his hands, to communicate his thoughts by words, and to record his ideas so that others may read them.

It is true that many animals have some natural abilities that are better than like abilities that man has. For example, some animals have unusually keen senses of hearing, sight, taste, smell, and touch, and even intuition. An eagle is able to see much farther than a man can see, but man has overcome this handicap by making field glasses and telescopes. Birds can fly, but man has built artificial machines in which he flies higher and longer than birds can fly.

Man's power to think gives him responsibilities that are greater than those that God has given to the animals. Man must learn to control his thoughts and direct them along positive lines or he will suffer from worry, fear of the future, and other negative emotions that interfere with his well-being and harmonious human relationships. Man was created to be like his Father-God, and to have dominion over all things, but he often uses his brain and his power to think in ways that bring him responsibilities over which he finds it difficult to have dominion.

The power to laugh evidently has been given man to help him balance his disposition when his thoughts seem to get beyond his control. Laughter often becomes a safety valve that relieves tense states of mind in unpleasant situations that man causes through the unwise use of his intellect.

When we laugh, it is usually because some mental tension inside of us lets go, allowing our inner joy to express itself for a moment. We may believe that something outside us is making us laugh but our laughter is really the expression of the joy of the Lord within us trying to help us to adjust ourselves so that we will not become too top-heavy with negative thoughts.

We all need to laugh more. When a heated argument is in progress, if someone concerned in the argument is wise and tactful, he can often say something that will bring out a laugh and relieve the tension.

When man works himself up into a brainstorm of self-importance, a good laugh will often help him come down out of the storm cloud. It is good to laugh at ourselves sometimes.

True laughter of course comes from the Lord's joy within us. Of course some laughs are merely cynical laughs that arise from a sarcastic attitude. These are not true laughs and they are not helpful. We laugh heartily at funny things and feel relieved. The joy that God has put into our hearts must find expression through us if we are to become normal, happy children of God. If we can express our joy through smiles and laughter at the right time, our joy becomes contagious and spreads to others and helps release God's joy that is within them.

Some of our greatest statesmen in history have mastered difficult situations by telling a witty story at the right time. Sometimes a preacher can wake up sleepers in his audience by telling an incident that causes them to laugh. Their laughter serves to relax and open their minds so that they will better receive and benefit by his sermon.

We have no record of Jesus having laughed, but He spoke of joy a number of times. He said: "These things have I spoken unto you, that my joy may be in you, and *that* your joy may be made full." And again: "But now I come to thee; and these things I speak in the world, that they may have my joy made full in themselves."

When we laugh, we express one of our God-given powers, and our laughter helps us as well as other persons about us. A good laugh exerts a softening effect upon worry, fear, and tenseness, and upon all kinds of difficult situations where a number of persons are involved. Sometimes we may be faced with what seem to be discouraging failures in our life. By finding a funny side to the incident that makes us laugh, we can lift up our spirit and forgive ourselves.

We do not understand where the laugh comes from, nor why we laugh when we see or hear something that we call funny. It just seems to be a feeling that is beyond our control. Some persons laugh more heartily than others and some seem to be almost unable to control their laughter when something amuses them. It is good to laugh at our own troubles, but we should not laugh at the troubles of others. It is more blessed to laugh with someone than to laugh at him. Remember that helpful laughter springs from good humor rather than from malice or scorn. If we will remember that when we laugh we are expressing the joy of the Lord, we shall encourage the joy that is in us to come forth into greater expression.

Sometimes we laugh when we are surprised or when something turns out differently than we had expected. This laugh is a much better reaction than sullen disappointment in this type of situation. In the Psalms we read:

> "Be glad in Jehovah,
>   and rejoice, ye righteous;
> And shout for joy,
>   all ye that are upright in heart."

Although we do not need to laugh out loud or even to smile in order to feel the joy of the Lord, these outward expressions of joy are helpful in bringing added happiness into our own lives as well as into the lives of our friends.

Let us therefore be glad that we can laugh and express the joy of the Lord freely.

I am a radiant center of divine love.

A Prayer Drill

First Day. *Divine love is now working through me, adjusting all the details of my life.*

Second Day. *Divine love fills me with joy and health.*

Third Day. *Divine love helps me to solve all my problems.*

Fourth Day. *Divine love is the fulfilling of the law in my affairs.*

Fifth Day. *Divine love draws prosperity to me.*

Sixth Day. *Divine love protects me from all harm.*

Seventh Day. *Divine love abides with me continually and satisfies my soul.*

Chapter 5

The Divine Order of Things

There is nothing lost in Spirit.

You and Your Past

THE present is eternal; it is always with us. It has always been with us and it will always be with us. Therefore the present is of more importance to you and to me than either the past or the future.

What we call the past lives only in our memory. It is true that our memory often reminds us of many good things and experiences happening in the past that we do not want to forget, but at the same time we must be careful that we do not let these memories rob the present moment of its opportunities and its vitality. We must not rest upon the past so comfortably that we have no desire to rise up and enjoy present blessings. We must not depend upon fond old memories for our present happiness.

Dreams of the past must not be allowed to blot out the reality of God's present blessings. Memories of past friendships must not crowd out the making and enjoyment of new friendships. Neither must past failures, mistakes, disappointments, or losses be allowed to intrude themselves upon our present life to dim its brightness and to interfere with today's success.

Remember that old things have passed away and that we are now in a new, glorious, vital world. The present is alive, fresh, and new because it belongs to God. Realize this and you will prove that the present is indeed sufficient for all your needs. If you have learned a lesson from an experience in the past, profit by that experience now, but do not waste any time in wishing that the past had been different. Do not admit that the past has any power over your present life. Do not allow yourself to be a "has-been," but be a "now-am."

We can profit by our past experiences to a certain degree, but we must not allow them to dominate or overshadow our present outlook. God is here now. He is our ever-living, ever-present source of good. Nothing that happened in the past can take Him away from us now. He is always with us, eternally new and good.

We may allow the past and future to rob us of our present joys and opportunities if we do not keep clearly in mind the Truth that now is the only time there is. At one time when the Jews were boasting that Abraham was their father, Jesus said, "Before Abraham was born, I am." Note that He said

"I am" and not "I was." When Jehovah spoke to Moses in the wilderness He identified Himself as "I AM THAT I AM." He did not say, "I was that I was."

Our ancestors have served us well, but we must not let them rule us. The man who has been successful but who now begins to live in memories of the past and to depend upon his successes in time gone by loses his ability to succeed today, because he fails to keep up with modern requirements of success. Success cannot live for long upon achievements of the past.

Grieving for losses in the past is not good either. God's present help heals the past. Things that were built in the past and are still with us are not in the past but belong to the present. Your home may have been built some time ago, but if it is of service to you now it is a part of the present.

Many things that had their beginning in the past and are useful now are a part of the present. Old thoughts about the past are the thieves that steal our present good. Material things are old or new according to the way we look at them. When the tombs of ancient Egypt are unearthed, they seem old because we associate old ideas with them. We think of them in connection with people who lived thousands of years ago, but the material in them is no older than the rocks that support the houses we are now living in.

A mummy in the museum is real now as a

mummy, but he lives in your mind as a man of ancient times. The museum today is filled with things of the present that represent ideas of the past. These ideas are in our mind and are recorded as ideas in books and on stones and parchments. The dusty mummy can have little influence upon our present life except through our thoughts about its past.

Jesus has great influence for good upon our present life because He lives today, not because He lived as a man two thousand years ago. Ideas of Truth live forever, but relative ideas grow stale and out of date.

It is not necessary for you to suffer under the cloud of a past experience. Remember that you are in the eternal sunshine of the present. Open your soul, your mind, and your heart to the present opportunities and live now. The past is gone; let it go gracefully. The present is here, and it is yours forever. Live it, find God in it, and be at peace.

> How can we keep the new year young
> And save ourselves from useless age?
> The way is clear for all who will.
> God's time is ever now, it has no past;
> The future cannot steal away its joy.
> Each day is new and fresh and clean
> To one who finds a new beginning in
>   each breath.

The Good Old Days

Roses are just as fragrant today as they were when you first smelled them in the garden of your childhood. If they are not so sweet to you as they used to be, do not blame the roses. Look to yourself and discover what you have lost that you now need, to reveal the present sweetness of the roses to you. You will find that the sweetness, or the lack of it, is really in your own mind.

The mind is capable of sweetening many things that we become aware of through the palate and through the nose. Through an appreciative state of mind, fruits, vegetables, flowers, and everything else that we use can be improved.

Some of us think of the days when life held more joy for us than it holds now. We yearn for the good in the past, forgetting that time spent in thinking about the past is largely wasted. We dwell on the excellence of the past because we do not know how to appreciate the good in the present. The fact is that there never was more good at any time in the past than there is right now. "Now is the acceptable time."

We are held back in our present progress when we try to live again in the experiences of the past. We as a race have unwisely let our ancestors dominate us. They plan our bodily health and mold our characters. We let them do these things because we take it for granted that they knew how to live aright. We have much to learn about life before we can really begin to live, and before we can begin to learn to live, we have much of ancestral precedent to unlearn. We should be growing toward perfection instead of building upon the haphazard foundation laid by our ancestors.

Our ancestors inherited certain characteristics from their ancestors, and we calmly accept these characteristics as they are passed on to us—frail bodies that last at best but three score years and ten, and that are subject meanwhile to all kinds of diseases, and emotional natures dominated by hatred, lust, greed, envy, fear, discouragement, and the like. We accept them in the belief that they belong to the normal man and woman. Our ancestors experienced many unpleasant things and, in their ignorance, tolerated them, but the fact that they did so cannot possibly prove that these things are normal. We would not accept from our ancestors an inheritance of personal property consisting of rags and rubbish. We do not need to accept from them a negative heritage in our minds and bodies if we do not choose to do so.

The way to refuse an undesirable inheritance is to deny that you are a child of the flesh. Deny that you inherit weakness, lust, fear, disease, or any other negative thing from your ancestors, and affirm your inheritance from your heavenly Father, which includes life, health, joy, peace, purity, and harmony. These are yours for the asking. If you ask for them and believe in them and use them, then you are truly an heir of God. "Call no man your father on the earth: for one is your Father, *even* he who is in heaven."

We can never make real progress in self-mastery until we break away from the dominance of our ancestors and of the past in general. We thoughtlessly believe in and do many foolish things merely because our ancestors did them and believed in them.

The whole array of troubles, hardships, wars, sin, and death is a relic of the blunders of our ancestors, who, instead of depending on God, their Father, ignorantly relied on their own strength to solve their problems.

We must learn to deny the power of our ancestors over us and must think of God as our Father. When we do this, we shall break away from a vast accumulation of mental and physical error that has been holding us down, and we shall then find in our new freedom possibilities of growth and life that we never before dreamed of.

There are no "good old days." Today, if you find God in it, is the best day that you have ever lived.

"Little Mister My"

Most of us have a personality in us that we might call "Little Mister My." We should keep our eye on him to see that he does not get out of hand. His favorite pastime is to lay hold of certain things and in his possessive way set them apart for his own personal benefit. These things may or may not have monetary value. They may be material things, persons, or ideas, but whatever they may be, they are held under the personal domination of "Little Mister My."

This little fellow's point of view proves to be quite shortsighted, for he expects these things to serve him well while they are bound by him. His possessiveness smothers the very breath of God in these things which he holds too tightly in his mental grasp.

"Little Mister My" often limits our capacity for friendship, good will, and peace of mind. He would sacrifice our friends, our peace of mind, and our success for things as trivial as a slip of printed paper representing money. True happiness and peace of mind actually depend upon the sharing and releasing of possessions so that they can move in the spirit of divine order to bless others also. When the little personality in you holds things so tightly that they cannot become active helpers who would serve you under God's free law, they are bound to become helpless liabilities to him.

When things are bound in the world by the grasp of personal possessiveness, they cannot perform the helpful service that they could if they were shared with God. Do not let "Little Mister My" sell you on the idea that you can prosper by binding things to you. When you bind things to you, you squeeze the life out of them and out of your spiritual nature and drive friendships, happiness, peace of mind, and prosperity away from you.

The things of the world are necessary and good when they are left free to serve God and man. But when a man tries to limit them to serve himself alone they will fail him. When he sets them free to serve God, his mind will also be free to share in God's abundance of spiritual things, which will bring happiness to him.

When you permit "Little Mister My" to hold onto certain things, or to some person as belonging only to you, the things or the person are not free to express God's love, good will, and generosity toward you. Love, good will, generosity, forgiveness—these are of the kingdom of heaven, and we bind these heavenly things so far as we are concerned when we bind the earthly things through which they are expressed. When we free the things on our earth, we also free and condition our consciousness so that we can receive the good things of the kingdom of heaven.

Jesus said to His disciples: "Verily I say unto you,

What things soever ye shall bind on earth shall be bound in heaven; and what things soever ye shall loose on earth shall be loosed in heaven." And He went on to say: "If two of you shall agree on earth as touching anything that they shall ask, it shall be done for them of my Father who is in heaven."

You will notice that "Little Mister My" in you has difficulty in agreeing with other persons concerning the possession of things, and you therefore cannot cooperate with another person in asking the Father who is in heaven for good things.

When there is disagreement, ill feeling, and condemnation in the little "My" personality of a person, it is useless for him to ask the Father for anything. These negative conditions block God's loving answer, which comes swiftly when they are replaced by agreement, good will, and forgiveness. Peter came to Jesus and said to Him: "Lord, how oft shall my brother sin against me, and I forgive him? until seven times? Jesus saith unto him, I say not unto thee, Until seven times; but, Until seventy times seven."

We must not allow misunderstandings concerning material things to prevent us from finding God. Before we can pray effectively, we must forgive and release all people and things that we have bound on earth. "Little Mister My" must not be allowed to assert himself selfishly, but he must learn that the name of his better self is really "Big Mister Our."

"Mister Our" generously releases things as he says: "It is my pleasure to share God's good things." When "Mister My" learns his real name, "Mister Our," he will agree with his fellowmen and will set all things and all people free to do the will of God. God in His kingdom will then reward him freely by opening the windows of heaven to pour out blessings to him. When "Little Mister My" learns that he cannot lose anything that he releases to God, he will be willing to share all things, because he will be able to understand what Jesus meant when He said, "All things that are mine are thine, and thine are mine."

Conquest

I fought an enemy in righteous wrath
And by sheer strength and hate
I brought him crying to his knees;
I vanquished him by mortal power,
But he my enemy remained
    unchanged in heart.
I fought an enemy with love and faith,
And by my love and kindness
Overcame his grudge.
I vanquished him by power divine,
And changed him from a foe to friend
    of mine.

You and Your Future

Your future is bound up in your present. What you are thinking and doing and being today is the pattern of what you will be thinking and doing and being tomorrow. If you would make tomorrow better than yesterday, change the things you do today.

Today is yesterday's tomorrow. How do you like the experiences you are having today? Are they as good as you counted on their being yesterday? Yesterday did you look for tomorrow to be so much better than yesterday that you slighted yesterday? Are you making the same mistake today and slighting today's opportunities because you are dreaming of tomorrow's possibilities?

This moment brings you many rich opportunities. It holds the key to the success of your future moments. This key is your right appreciation and cooperation with the source of your success now. If you seek the source of your spiritual good today, you will lay a firm foundation for the manifestation of your good tomorrow.

Actually there is no tomorrow, for today is always here. If you waste today, you waste tomorrow. When you put off your good until tomorrow, you are placing it beyond your reach. Take it now while you can and cultivate it, and it will grow so that you will be able to harvest its increase when tomorrow becomes today.

It is proper to plan ahead, but all successful planning must be founded upon an appreciation of present opportunities. Many persons feel that the present is a blank but that the future holds riches and honor for them. They fail to see the good things at hand today because their mental gaze is focused upon the future. Worrying about the future will not promote your success, and it will take the joy out of your present. The present must be well lived, blessed, and improved, for tomorrow is dependent upon it. Do not quarrel with the present, for it is your faithful, generous friend who will respond richly to your love and appreciation.

Do not delay getting acquainted with the possibilities of your ever-present friend. Perhaps the greatest of these possibilities is your opportunity for getting acquainted with the Christ within you. Do not postpone this thrilling experience till a more convenient season. Do not put off the enjoyment of your spiritual blessings until tomorrow. You do not defer sleeping, eating, or breathing until tomorrow. Remember that your sustenance does not depend entirely upon the material food you eat, for you are also nourished by the inspiration of the Spirit. Every word proceeding out of the mouth of God helps to sustain you and keep you well and happy. Without this spiritual food your soul would starve. Eat the soul-nourishing bread of God's living Word freely every day and you will live more abundantly.

It is no wonder that so many people feel dissatisfied with life. They are so because they try to live on material food alone. They put off eating the real spiritual food of life till the future. They are spiritually hungry and they do not realize what is the matter with them.

You can begin today to enjoy the bread of life and by eating it with your mind you will fill your life with joy, peace, love, and harmony. Do not put off the enjoyment of these good things until tomorrow. Begin enjoying them at once.

Jesus said, "Seek ye first his kingdom, and his righteousness; and all these things shall be added unto you." He also said, "The kingdom of God is within you." He did not mean that it is within your material body but that the ability to contact the spiritual kingdom lies within you. The kingdom of God is within the spiritual man. As you search diligently for God within your heart, you will find Him.

Christ, the perfect Son of God, is the spiritual foundation of your being. It is only through this Christ that you will be able to know God. Christ is standing at the door of your consciousness knocking. Why not open the door today and let Him in? Begin today to live the life more abundant. Christ manifested through Jesus announced that He came that we might have life and have it more abundantly. That abundant life is omnipresent and it is waiting for you to enjoy it. It is the very body of Christ. Take it, eat it, drink it, and be filled with it today. Since there is no tomorrow, you must do it today.

It is not a good idea to spend much time in boasting of the good that you have done in the past. It is better to let your present goodness speak for itself.

Remember that while marshaling your forces in a repetition of a past victory, you are leaving your present weak points unguarded.

In praising yourself for past achievements you are exalting your personality. As the personality is exalted as a thing apart from God, you are separated from the one source of all power.

You can increase your present usefulness by depending upon God for your strength and ability. Today is the only day that concerns you.

It is right and proper to believe that through the Spirit of Truth within you can do all things, but it is a mistake to be puffed up with pride on account of this fact.

There is no greater hindrance to a man's spiritual growth than his holding to the reality of past achievements and family traditions.

The past is a hard, stern reality to those who believe in it, and it enfolds its devotees in a stifling little shell that prevents their souls from soaring into the greater possibilities of the present.

There is nothing lost in Spirit.

A Prayer Drill

First Day. *I dwell in the kingdom of peace and harmony today.*

Second Day. *No mistake of the past can disturb me today, for God's omnipresent love has wiped away all of the unpleasant things of the past.*

Third Day. *No past joy can steal my present joy from me, for joy is eternal.*

Fourth Day. *No loss of the past can take anything away from my present store of good things, for God with all His substance is here now.*

Fifth Day. *No sin of the past can torment me, for old things have passed away, and I am a new creature in Christ Jesus.*

Sixth Day. *Today is real and vital, for it is filled with God's life, substance, love, and joy.*

Seventh Day. *I have let go of all outworn thoughts of the past, and I am being inspired with ideas of Truth by the Spirit of Truth.*

Chapter 6

God Everywhere

I greet the presence and power of God here.

How to Find Heaven Everywhere

MAN is like a squirrel in a cage so long as he accepts as real conditions as they appear to be in the world about him. He does a lot of running after happiness, but he does not seem to catch up with it. Progress toward the heaven where happiness abounds cannot be attained by distance run nor by attaining worldly influence, wealth, or power.

Things are really not what they appear to be. For instance, an object nearby appears to be large, but at a distance it seems to be small. Traveling along a country road, we stop under the shade of a mighty oak, which towers above us splendidly. But as we drive on it seems to grow smaller and smaller until finally it is only a tiny speck on the distant horizon, and then it disappears entirely. We realize that nothing has happened to the tree, which is still tall and sturdy. We know that the changes in its appearance are due to our change of viewpoint.

God is like the oak tree. When we get close to Him, He covers us with His protecting love, but when we turn away from Him, His power seems to grow less. We realize that God does not really change, but still we allow appearances to confuse us and cause us to lose faith in His omnipresent power to help us. We cannot change God but we can change our position in relation to Him.

Troubles are not material things. They are mistaken ideas about things. Troubles come to us when we are too close to things and too far from God. When we draw close to blessings by counting them, they grow larger, but when we turn our attention to our troubles, our blessings seem to grow less. Paul advised: "Whatsoever things are true, whatsoever things are honorable, whatsoever things are just, whatsoever things are pure, whatsoever things are lovely, whatsoever things are of good report; if there be any virtue, and if there be any praise, think on these things."

Why is it important to follow Paul's advice? Because we become like that which we think about. We enter heaven by centering our attention upon heaven.

There is the true, good world that God made out of pure spiritual substance by His word, and there is the changeable good-and-evil world that man makes out of thought substance. These two worlds are both here in our presence waiting for us to choose between them.

Your thoughts precede your actions. Through the right process of thinking you can bring all your affairs into God's good world where all is well.

A motion-picture screen impartially reflects horrible pictures of destruction or scenes of beauty, pictures faithfully portraying human woe or human joy, whichever the mind of man elects to throw upon it. Like a motion-picture screen the natural world reflects either the perfection and beauty of God's heaven or the double world of human misunderstanding. Whatever a man has faith in and concentrates his attention upon, this will be his portion.

God is not far away; His love is very close to you at all times. When you make loving, living, God-filled thoughts your daily companions, God's Spirit will pervade your life and the tree of life will overshadow you. When you have faith in God's omnipresent life, you draw very close to the tree of life. Its power and glory are as real to you as the great oak by the roadside is real to the traveler who stands close to it. But if your thoughts are filled with troubles you stand under the tree of good-and-evil and from that doubting viewpoint the tree of life appears to be but a speck upon the horizon.

Things are not what they seem to be. They are

what you make them by your thinking. God has prepared a beautiful place for you in the invisible realm very close to you. You can move into this beautiful realm without changing your street number. In fact the place where you eat and sleep has little control over it. But the character of your thoughts has a great deal to do with your chance of entering it.

As you draw near to God through prayer and meditation, He draws near to you. Prayer is one of the processes of right thinking. Draw near to evil and it will meet you halfway also. No airplane can travel fast enough or far enough to take you any closer to heaven than you are now. Only on the wings of your inner true thoughts can you reach the kingdom of heaven. And when you find the kingdom of heaven within you, all the good things of life will be added unto you.

Remember that God is with you when you are with Him. He is with you now if you believe that He is. Therefore stop thinking foolish thoughts of doubt and worry, which carry you away from heaven, and begin thinking God's thoughts of faith and assurance. Make yourself secure by dwelling in thought upon the reality of God's perfect creation, and take your thoughts away from worry about man's topsy-turvy, good-and-evil world. Live now, and enjoy the kingdom of heaven now.

"The kingdom of heaven is at hand." It is within

you. Enter into it with joy, thanksgiving, and praise today, no matter if the world about you may seem to be all wrong. Remember the words of the Psalmist and rejoice:

"If I make my bed in Sheol, behold, thou art there."

Unity

Unity is the greatest need of the world today.

Need for it is mentioned in the newspapers and magazines every day. Unity is needed in politics, in human relations, in religion, in business, and in national and international affairs. *Unity* means "concord, harmony, accord."

Many workers may be engaged in doing a certain job, and these workers may have a diversity of opinions about many subjects, but even so they can work together harmoniously as long as they are unified in the common purpose of doing a good job.

There may be several political parties in the field, but they can meet in unity when they agree that they all love the same country and sincerely work to serve and promote the best interests and welfare of their fellow citizens.

There are many religions in the world, but there is no need of the members of one religious group quarreling with the members of another religious group. All can cooperate in the common purpose of doing something to promote the spiritual welfare of the followers of their own group, even though the groups may have quite different religious beliefs and methods of worship.

A better understanding among all sincere religious groups will promote unity and good will. Love is the magic-working power that must be employed to create the better understanding.

When we see the wonders of the universe about us, we must conclude that there is an intelligent power pervading it, which created man and now cares for his material and spiritual welfare. It matters not what we call this power. A name cannot change it. Jesus called it "God" and "the Father." All worshipers of a power higher than themselves can work together to promote good will, harmony, and peace among themselves. If we find ourselves unable to love a certain person, we should be able to love the power that gives him life.

The universe and all things in it are manifestly held together by an intelligent power, which functions to maintain unity and harmony in its operation. We Truth students like to think of this intelligent power as God's love.

Jesus pointed a way for us to become consciously unified with this power by saying that the greatest commandment is to love God with all our soul, mind, and strength. In order to care for so many creatures this infinite power of love must be omnipresent whether we are aware of its presence or not. If it were not now enfolding us, we should not be here. There would be nothing to hold our body together.

The universe did not just happen to be. Even the human body, with its intricate cells, organs, and its ability to grow, proves that there is a superpresence of intelligence and harmony at work in it. We must conclude that God must have great love for all of us when we realize that His life pervades us and provides us with love, air, and sunshine, while at the same time we are freely permitted to take or leave as much of these blessings as we will.

How wonderful it would be if every one of us could appreciate and enjoy with full understanding the gifts that God is trying to give us! If we would accept more of His love, we must express more of it in our thoughts, words, and actions. When we learn to express more of God's love, greater harmony will become manifest in our affairs.

Many of us today are thinking that if other people would be more peaceful and loving it would be possible for us to be more peaceful and loving. We may think something like this: "When others are ready to do their part, I shall be ready to do mine." But this attitude cannot solve the problem of disharmony, because others are perhaps saying the same thing about us. The fact is that the only person who can change my world is me myself. It will do little good for us to wait for someone else to save the world. The beginning of unity and harmony in our world is in our own hands.

What you yourself think and do sets up the pattern for unity and harmony in your world.

The whole world is waiting to see what you are going to do. God has placed a great responsibility on you, for He has given you authority over all things in your world. When you consciously establish your unity with God through love, you open the way for a certain degree of harmonious cooperation between yourself and all persons. You may not understand or appreciate your next-door neighbor's desires, ideals, or problems, or agree with his religion or politics, but when you strengthen your unity with God through practicing love to God you begin to understand your neighbor better, because the same God who is in you is in him also.

God is your neighbor's life, even though your neighbor may not realize God's presence. Therefore when you unify yourself with the God power that is in you, you also unify yourself with the God power that is in your neighbor. Though he may not consciously know God as you do, nevertheless God knows him and is with him, giving him as much good as your neighbor is able to receive. Of course God could help this neighbor a great deal more if he would cooperate with God more definitely by expressing more of God's love.

God gives His love to help His children as a human father extends his hand to help his little child over a rough road. But the child must put forth his hand and clasp his father's hand if his father is to steady his steps. So our heavenly Father extends His hand of love to us, and we take hold of it by clasping it in love. We must love God sincerely if His love is to work perfectly in our behalf. We can establish our unity with God's love more firmly by loving Him more sincerely. By loving God more sincerely, we also establish a greater degree of unity between ourselves and Him and all people. Even though many people may not yet have consciously learned to work in cooperation with God's love, nevertheless His love is with them and is having a certain influence over them that may be unknown to them, but the Truth is that their very life depends upon His love.

As you learn to love God more dearly, you experience an increasing love toward all persons. Instead of condemning those who are falling short of your ideals, you will see by the light of your greater love new ways to help them by sending your thoughts of healing, harmony, peace, and good will to them. They need help because their negative thoughts and actions can bring them only disappointments.

Unloving thoughts create conditions that will fall into oblivion of their own weight. In the end only Truth, unity, harmony, and peace will endure. We must help people everywhere to think thoughts that endure and bring to pass life, joy, and peace.

The whole world is waiting for you and me to express our unity with God's love. Let us no longer think, "Let somebody else start the millennium, and I will try to follow him." Everyone who reads this may start a new spiritual wave of peace on earth today if he will begin now to practice loving God all day long every day. This great opportunity is waiting for any person who is willing to make a business of loving God. By expressing each day more love to God, you will discover that love is the key that unlocks the door to God's kingdom.

Heaven is indeed within the heart of every man, but each man must discover heaven for himself. Here within himself he will find his unity with God and with all men.

God Will Help You Do Your Work

You will have no more hard tasks when you let God help you in everything you undertake. He will change your difficult assignments into joyous adventures that will bring good results to you and to all concerned.

You probably know from experience that when you like your work, you can produce more and better results with less fatigue. The hardest work that you can do is that which you dislike or are not interested in.

The quality and quantity of the work that you accomplish by your own physical efforts without God's help is often restricted by the brakes that you clamp on them by your own negative thoughts of worry, hurry, disapproval, and the like. Did you ever try to drive your car when you had forgotten to release the brakes? It did not perform very well under this condition, did it? Neither will your efforts to do your work progress smoothly when you put the brakes on them by feeling resistant toward your work.

Even when you like your work, it will not seem easy if, in doing it, you depend entirely on your own physical and mental efforts without relying on the guidance of a higher power.

When we do our work without the help of God, we work outside the Garden of Eden, as Father Adam did long ago when he refused to work in harmony with the divine principles. Adam chose to do his own will instead of God's will and ate the fruit of the tree of knowledge of good and evil. His disobedience put him in a position where he had to work and earn his living by the sweat of his brow. He therefore had to endure all kinds of hardships.

God did not plan such a life for man. He prepared the Garden of Eden for man to enjoy while he dressed it and kept it. So long as Adam was obedient to the laws of the Garden, all was well with him. I feel sure that the Garden of Eden can be entered again at any time by any man who will become obedient to God's laws concerning the Garden, if he will cooperate with God in all that he does instead of insisting on doing his own will.

By conforming to the Christ principles in all that he thinks and does, a man is really praying without ceasing. When we realize that great things are accomplished not by might nor by power but by the Spirit of the Lord, all our work becomes easier and there is no mental strain in it. Jesus reminded His followers that it was the Father within Him that did the mighty works, and Moses told the Children of Israel when they were hard pressed by the Egyptians to stand still and see the salvation of the Lord. We can be diligent and happy in our daily work and our efforts will not fail if we let God's mighty will be done in and through us.

We can enter the Garden of Eden and live in it while still living in the house where we are now. Our house will be surrounded by a different kind of mental and spiritual atmosphere. Our neighbors will perhaps not be able to understand the meaning of the change in spiritual atmosphere, but they will surely see the improved results in our life and in our affairs.

The Garden-of-Eden consciousness is very much

like the kingdom-of-heaven consciousness, which Jesus has instructed us to pray for in the Lord's Prayer. In this prayer we pray that the kingdom-of-heaven consciousness may come into the world and be in it as it is in heaven. This means that the kingdom will come into the world of any individual who complies with its principles, even though his neighbors are not aware of the kingdom. It can become a reality to any man if he will comply with its principles.

Jesus has taught us to pray not only for the kingdom of heaven to come, but also for our daily bread and for the forgiveness of our debts, which, according to the divine law, requires that we forgive others their debts before we can be forgiven ours. The teachings of Jesus in regard to applying the divine principles are that we must comply with these principles by using them. We must do to others as we would have them do to us. We must be peaceful if we expect to find peace. We must be loving if we would receive love. We must forgive if we expect to be forgiven. We must give if we would receive.

We must overcome evil with good. We must be generous. We must be meek, yet firm in faith and steadfast in purpose. When we stand firm in the Christ consciousness of forgiveness and understanding, we do not condemn those who disagree with us. All these musts can be summed up in these words: "We must keep our eye single to the good and not experiment with good and evil."

It is said that it takes two to make a quarrel. If this be true, there can be no quarrel when one of the two maintains his spiritual poise. The other fellow may lose his poise, but since he is only one of a necessary two, there can be no quarrel when the first one refuses to quarrel.

Sometimes it may seem to us that if we do not fight we may lose our shirt, but we should remember that the Lord has plenty of shirts to give us when we work in harmony with His laws. Jesus said: "If any man would . . . take away thy coat, let him have thy cloak also." A coat or a cloak or a shirt is too unimportant a thing to provoke us and cause us to be cast out of the Garden of Eden.

When we cooperate with God in Spirit and in Truth, our actions also become harmonious with our thoughts. Adam did not eat of the forbidden fruit until he had first decided to do so in his mind. We do the wrong things first in our mind before we do them with our hands. Therefore the Christ teachings must first be accepted and followed in our thoughts, and then our deeds will fall in line with our good thoughts.

When we follow the Shepherd, He shows us the easy way, and He protects us. He leads us beside the still waters and over smooth paths. He keeps us from harm. He is ever with us, but if we do not follow Him but choose our own way, we may find ourselves in the byways, which are filled with thistles, rocks, and difficulties; also there may be wolves waiting to devour us.

When we follow Him, we tread the smooth path, where our tasks are easy and our bread is waiting for us each day. When we follow the divine Shepherd as He guides us, all our ways are ways of pleasantness and all our paths are paths of peace.

The Unity of All Things

Unity in Spirit is the goal that all men are seeking to attain. Few of us realize that this is our ultimate divine goal in life, although most of us do agree that there is strength in unity and that "united we stand, divided we fall." The principle underlying the strength that is found in unity applies also to the unification of the departments of an individual's being as well as to the harmonious unification of the people in a nation.

There is more to man than we perceive with our senses, for he is really a threefold being made up of Spirit, mind, and body. When these three departments of a man's being are united in purpose and understanding, he will be able to understand and profit by the full and deeper meaning set forth in the life and teachings of Jesus Christ.

Even the disciples of Jesus sometimes found His sayings difficult to understand, because spiritual experiences cannot be clearly described in worldly language. Jesus therefore often used parables to help make the meaning of His teachings clearer.

The following words, which Jesus spoke to His disciples concerning their spiritual nature and their relationship to God, were hard for them to comprehend intellectually. "If ye abide in me, and my words abide in you, ask whatsoever ye will, and it shall be done unto you." Here Jesus was referring to the spiritual nature of man's unity with the Father. Words are inadequate to describe such things.

Jesus explained that His teachings could be successfully applied by all persons who would comply with the spiritual laws of being. He did not limit their application to His disciples, for He said: "Neither for these only do I pray, but for them also that believe on me through their word; that they may all be one; even as thou, Father, *art* in me, and I in thee, that they also may be in us."

He described a spiritual state of unity between God and man that is beyond the understanding of the worldly-minded individual. Jesus spoke in the following words of the glory of Christ, who is the perfect spiritual man, created in the image and likeness of God: "And the glory which thou hast given me I have given unto them; that they may be one, even as we *are* one. . . . Thou lovedst me before the foundation of the world."

Jesus is often referred to as our Elder Brother, and so He proved Himself to be, for He set an example before us to show us how we may also reach the divine goal of unity. He did this by lifting up His mind and body and unifying them with His spiritual Christ Self in God. All men must eventually follow Jesus' example and demonstrate their oneness with Christ in God. Our goal is to become spiritually aware of our oneness as Spirit, soul, and body in our own being and also aware of our oneness with God and Christ, as Jesus did. The Christ, speaking through Jesus, said: "I and the Father are one."

Jesus came to show us that we are also one with God and His perfect Son, Christ, and that we can become aware of our unity by believing that we do live in Spirit and in Truth with Christ in God.

In the world about us we find many good people who believe that mind and body are the whole man. They may have been told that each man has a Spirit or a spiritual nature, but they are not greatly interested in their Spirit because they cannot see it. The needs of their minds and bodies take their entire attention, so they have no time left to give to spiritual matters. There is therefore lack of unity in the lives of these people. Their thoughts and actions are guided only by the material things of the world. They have no understanding of their Spirit, nor of Spirit, which animates and cares for the whole creation. By thinking only about the things of the world, and believing that man is only a physical

being, they separate their physical nature from their
spiritual Self, and also from God!

Man must realize unity in his being before he
can enjoy the fullness of life that was promised by
Jesus Christ. Jesus overcame the last enemy, death,
by resurrecting His body. He was then able to unify
His Spirit, mind, and body with God in perfect
order.

When we believe the Truth about spiritual man,
we gain an understanding that transcends the
world's standard of thinking. We shall then be able
consciously to abide in Christ as He abides in us.
When more and more of God's children awaken as
Jesus did to the reality of their unity with God
through the Christ within them, they will bring
about a new form of unity in the conditions of the
manifest world. This unity will pervade all the
peoples of the world and help them to find a spirit
of love and good will among them that will prevent
future war and strife.

A man need not separate himself from the world
of manifest things in order to be able to enter into
the kingdom of heaven. He can bring heaven into
his manifest world by unifying his mind and body
with Christ. He will then be able to find God
within himself and also within his neighbors.

As man becomes unified with God through his
own spiritual nature, he beholds God in all things,
for in reality there is no separation between the

manifest world and God's Spirit. Belief in separation exists only in the minds of men who are spiritually blind because they have not yet quickened their faith to believe that God is everywhere present in Spirit in them and in the world. Those who are spiritually blind and who can see only the world of appearances may think that heaven must be somewhere else, perhaps in the sky, because they cannot see it with their physical eyes.

Jesus has taught us to pray: "Thy kingdom come. Thy will be done in earth, as it is in heaven." When we lift our thoughts up to a place where we abide in Christ and He in us, we shall realize that we are already in the kingdom of heaven right here on earth.

When we become unified in our own being—Spirit, soul, and body—we find our unity with God. When we attain this understanding, we are able to see all nations and all people in our world unified. Through our inner unity our spiritual eyes are opened to Truth and we see our world perfect as God created it.

Those who will not accept the Truth that they are one with Christ in God will of course remain in a world that has trials, troubles, unhappiness, death, and destruction, because they see only in part. But those who see with the eyes of Spirit will see all things in their right relationship.

God's perfect creation includes matter as well as

Spirit. When we look only at the material aspects of life, we behold only a part of God's creation. Christ within us will help us to see the spiritual creation that pervades the material manifestations of God's perfect creation, namely, the kingdom of God on our earth, even if our next-door neighbors have not yet progressed spiritually to the extent that they too can see it.

The man who dwells in the kingdom of heaven will have no arguments or difficulties with his neighbors, for he sees and understands the love of God as the reality in the unity of Spirit. Therefore, he knows that that which is discordant in the material world is not the whole picture but is only a partial view of true conditions and has no power to harm God's whole, perfect universe, which includes unity of all things in God's perfection.

I greet the presence and power of God here.

A Prayer Drill

First Day. *Through the activity of the Christ Mind, all the earth is unified in God's goodness.*

Second Day. *In the unity of the Christ Spirit all men are one in God's love.*

Third Day. *The magic-working power of God's love is dissolving all discord in the world.*

Fourth Day. *The light of Christ Truth is breaking upon the whole world, revealing the love of God in every heart.*

Fifth Day. *All men are one in Christ, and peace and harmony fill the land.*

Sixth Day. *I am ready to express God's love now. I shall not wait for others to act first.*

Seventh Day. *There is but one presence and one power in the universe. This presence and power is God, the good Creator of all things.*

Chapter 7

The Words We Speak

**No man cometh unto me
save the Father send him.**

Let Something Good Be Said

WE should all consider well what Jesus said about the use of words, for He points the way to mastery of them. Here is His loving advice: "I say unto you, that every idle word that men shall speak, they shall give account thereof in the day of judgment. For by thy words thou shalt be justified, and by thy words thou shalt be condemned."

Since God created all things by His word and since man, His son, was created in His image and likeness and given dominion over things on the earth, it must follow that man's words have creative power also.

God's words are constructive and creative, but man has acquired the bad habit of speaking destructive words. Jesus realized that men were using words in negative ways, and no doubt that is the reason why He gave advice and warning concerning their use. He knew that man lives by words, for He said: "Man shall not live by bread alone, but by every word that proceedeth out of the mouth of God."

Jesus' own words were powerful because they were backed by His faith in the Father. His words healed the sick, fed the multitudes, cast out demons, and raised the dead.

Too many of us today are using words that harm us. We might just as well be speaking words that are constructive, that build up our inner power and joy and that harmonize our outer affairs. Because we are justified or condemned by the words we speak, we should recognize the great responsibility that goes with our power of speech. Because our words are the expression of our thoughts, we must control our thoughts as well as our words and guide them into fruitful expression.

It is important to note how our words uplift or depress our loved ones. I have known cases where one member of a family weakened and depressed another member by his well-meant but negative words of sympathy. A husband undermined his wife's courage and lessened her will to get well when he sympathetically continued to call her "poor thing." His words encouraged her to believe that she was in a hopeless state of health. He told her how sorry he was for her, and he explained to his friends in detail how she suffered and how hopeless her case was. His words, which were meant to be kind and helpful, were really cruel and hurtful, because they emphasized the condition that they both wanted healed.

Everyone will find it well worth his while to practice saying words that are in harmony with God's creative words. God did not belittle the things He had created; He blessed them and saw that they were very good. When we think of God as seeing all His creations as very good, and when we try to follow His example by also seeing all things as good, we shall join with Him in bringing His perfect creation into manifestation in our life and affairs. Jesus Christ admonished: "Ye therefore shall be perfect, as your heavenly Father is perfect."

We must not allow outer appearances to trick us into saying words that are destructive or untrue of God's creation. Many times every day most people speak idle words. They do not realize that by doing so they are asking for things and conditions to come into their life that they do not want.

The affirmations of Truth that are given in this book and in other Unity literature are intended to help readers direct their words into constructive channels. An affirmation is a statement of Truth to be spoken by the reader in an effort to correct negative conditions in his body and affairs. Truth affirmations also train him to form the habit of speaking constructive words instead of careless, negative ones.

Why should man use the wonderful power intrusted to him by his Creator to destroy his own happiness and peace of mind, which are part of the good world that God created for him? Let us think more seriously about the words we speak.

We do not need to fear negative words; rather we should learn to love constructive words and use them to bring good to ourselves. Instead of being afraid of negative words, we should be courageous as we stand firmly with God in speaking good words, words that create about us a world that is in accord with the perfect world that He created in the beginning. By the use of creative, good words, we can bring the manifestation of God's good world into our life experience. This will be the coming of the kingdom of heaven onto our earth.

We should not allow our human sympathy to trick us into saying negative words. If we really love someone and truly want to help him we must speak positive words of encouragement to him, words of love, strength, and courage. We should not ease him off into a negative limbo of discouragement and sadness by our slushy, negative words of sadness and depression.

If You Like It, Say So

It seems only fair that we should make acknowledgment of the good that comes our way. We should not just take for granted the blessings that we receive, whether they come from God or man.

When we gratefully acknowledge a gift, we complete the transaction by doing our part. If we do not acknowledge a gift, we fail to do our part.

If your wife prepares a good meal for you and you eat it in silence without comment, you miss an opportunity to promote harmony and good will in your home. No doubt you enjoyed the food but not as much as you would have had you told the little woman that you liked it.

Your acknowledgment of a good service done you is a prosperity affirmation. Seriously ask for something and you may get it, but make an affirmation of thanks for it as already received in Spirit and you are sure to receive it in manifest form.

Unity teaches that an affirmative thanksgiving prayer is more effective than a begging prayer. Jesus tells us to pray as though we have already received. As a matter of fact God has prepared for us every good thing we need before we ask Him for it. When we make an affirmation acknowledging the good that we desire, we bring ourselves into touch with the good that He has already prepared. Our prayers are really answered even before we ask, but we must have faith enough to give thanks for them to render ourselves fit to appreciate and accept the good things that God is more willing to give than we are to receive.

Truth affirmations are made in a positive manner because they state what is true in God's perfect creation. When we affirm, "God is my health," we are speaking the Truth about God and ourselves as children of God. Even though our physical body may not seem to measure up to our affirmation, we should acknowledge what is true of God and His perfect kingdom if we wish that kingdom to come onto our earth.

Our acknowledgment brings the good that God has created in the realm of Spirit down into manifestation in our life. We can help God answer our prayer by making a positive acknowledgment of His power and goodness. It requires true faith to acknowledge what God has done for us before we can see it manifest in our life.

Grateful acknowledgment is an excellent way to receive in full measure the essence of God's good gift. When we accept and use a blessing that God gives us without making acknowledgment of it, we can enjoy it only to a limited degree. Nearly everyone accepts God's air as a matter of course, and does not think of its value unless his supply of air should be shut off and he be in danger of smothering. Then he realizes that air is the most valuable thing in his life, and he would be glad to exchange anything he possessed for it.

If we would give thanks to God every day for the air we breathe, we should enjoy our air more intensely. God's most precious gifts are poured out upon us every day and are seldom acknowledged by us. These include life, love, wisdom, power, peace, and harmony. If we would accept these with thanks, joy, and enthusiasm every day, we should be able to enjoy these blessings more fully, because we realize they are coming direct from our Father, God.

We can acknowledge the Truth that God is our life and our love by affirming that God is our life and our love. Affirming the Truth brings us closer to God's life and love. We become partners with God in making manifest His spiritual blessings in our life.

We can make an affirmation acknowledging the Truth of God's perfect creation in Spirit, even though our affairs do not seem to warrant it. Such an affirmation will lift us up into a better understanding of our unity with God, and will also open the way for His perfection to become manifest in our life.

Some devout men have thought that for a man to affirm perfection would be to tell a lie, because it would not be in accord with material facts. It is the appearance however that is deceiving us. God made only perfect things. When we harmonize ourselves with God's Truth by acknowledging it, then appearances must change to agree with God's Truth. When we have enough faith in God's power, love, and wisdom to affirm their omnipresent reality, then divine light begins to shine into our affairs and we shall see the Truth demonstrated there, proving that our affirmation was right.

Do not be afraid to acknowledge the receipt of that which God has given you in Spirit. Jesus said: "If ye abide in me, and my words abide in you, ask whatsoever ye will, and it shall be done unto you" and "According to your faith be it done unto you."

When we persist in acknowledging God's eternal, omnipresent goodness, even amid adverse appearances, our faith is proved by a demonstration of God's goodness in our life.

The Power of Praise

A praiseful attitude is like a well of living water bubbling up in your soul. It is pleasant, inspiring, and refreshing to you and to all persons you meet. It also stimulates the growth of good in your life.

Everyone and everything responds to sincere praise and is uplifted and blessed by it. Even plants and animals respond to heartfelt praise. They may not be able to understand your words, but they will be moved by the uplifting impulse that comes to them from your heart. Flowers grow better when they are praised; animals behave better and are more tractable when they are praised.

Children also are touched by true praise. True praise does not mean telling a child that he is better than another. True praise calls his attention to the good points that he has without comparing them with the poorer showing of another. A comparison often brings implied criticism of another person. This is not true but comparative praise.

Praise your work and you will find that it will become easier. Praise the organs of your body; your faithful heart; your marvelous digestive system; the wonderful cooling and heating system of your body that keeps it always at the same temperature.

It is good for us also to praise God and thank Him for guiding us with His infinite wisdom before we try to solve any problem or perform any duty that confronts us. When we praise God, we shall find that He is with us, ready to help us in all our ways. As we continue to praise God, we receive more power to praise not only God, but all things and all persons. When we praise God, we quicken our life by filling it with the power of God, which is the source of all power. God does not need our praise, but we need the spiritual lift that praising Him brings us. When we praise a person, we inspire him to a degree, but we also lift up something in ourselves which makes us happier, healthier, and more prosperous.

The sincere praise we feel and express in thoughts and words helps us in mind, body, and affairs. Daniel of old gave thanks to God and praised Him for revealing the king's dream and its interpretation

to him. Daniel did this before he went before the
king to recite the king's dream and its interpretation, something that all the sorcerers and soothsay-
ers of the realm were unable to do. Daniel was able
to contact God's wisdom through prayer, praise,
and giving thanks. We should praise God and thank
Him for revealing to us the solution to our problem
instead of worrying about it and wondering if we
shall be able to solve it.

The Psalms are filled with words of praise. In
Psalm 33:1, 3 (ASV) we read:

> "Rejoice in Jehovah, O ye righteous:
> Praise is comely for the upright. . . .
> Sing unto him a new song."

God is already infinitely wonderful whether we
praise Him or not, but when we praise Him, we do
something to ourselves. We lift ourselves up in consciousness to a better understanding and appreciation of His goodness, and as a result we are able to
enter more actively into His goodness and to sing a
new song. We can fill our life with radiance by
praising God.

It is a law of mind that we become more or less
like the kind of thoughts we think. When we allow
negative, critical thoughts to dominate our thinking, we acquire a negative outlook and lower ourselves into a realm where we cannot see the good

opportunities that lie before us. Such a procedure limits our happiness and our usefulness. But when we fill our mind with praiseful thoughts concerning God and the people we know, we acquire a new point of view and rise into a realm where we can see a new and more nearly perfect world about us. Old, negative things will pass away and even old, familiar, inanimate things in our surroundings will take on new beauty and present new possibilities of usefulness to us.

Praising others does not mean that we are to pour out words of flattery upon them. Flattery is not as spiritually effective as true praise. Sometimes it is better to praise a person silently rather than to stimulate his ego with spoken words. By praising the spiritual potentialities of a person who is traveling a negative path, we may help him to see enough light to guide him onto a path that will lead him toward more positive thought and action.

By understanding and rightly using our power of right thinking, we can rise above and pass over the rough places in our world as a pilot guides his airplane far above rough roads and swollen streams, and sails smoothly through the air where the uneven places in the earth are no longer problems. Praise is the lifting power in our life that can carry us above the seamy problems of our earthly experiences.

We may inspire others through our praise, but by praising we do even a greater service to ourselves than to those we praise. So when we meet obstacles and troubles in our world, let us rise above them by praising God and all His works. We do not always need to express our praise audibly, for silent thoughts and loving feelings of praise are quite effective.

Let us in consciousness rise on the wings of praise to a state where we can recognize and appreciate the spiritual beauty of the very kingdom of God, which is within us.

**No man cometh unto me
save the Father send him.**

A Prayer Drill

First Day. *I am not sustained by bread alone. I am sustained also by the living words proceeding out of the mouth of God.*

Second Day. *My words are Spirit, and they are life, and they bring me a good harvest of health, happiness, and prosperity.*

Third Day. *The Word of God now active in me heals, quickens, and strengthens my soul and body.*

Fourth Day. *"My mouth shall speak wisdom;
And the meditation of my heart
shall be of understanding."*

Fifth Day. *Let my thoughts and my words be in accord with Thy good words, my heavenly Father-God.*

Sixth Day. *My words shall spring from the inspiration of the Spirit of Truth and be filled with love, faith, joy, peace, courage, and health.*

Seventh Day. *My words are courageous and helpful when I listen for the promptings of God's still small voice within me before I speak.*

Chapter 8

No Barriers

**There is but one Presence
and one Power here.**

The Head of the House

EVERY household that has a wise, loving, harmonious, strong, sweet, and forgiving directive head is successful and happy. But since a single human being is seldom able to express all these good qualities at the same time, we should have very few successful, happy homes if there were not a higher Source from which a father or mother could receive assistance in managing the household.

However, no family head need be discouraged because of his or her inability to cope with the many problems that present themselves in rearing a family, for there is a divine Helper at hand who embodies all the needed qualities of leadership. No matter how lacking the human head of a family may seem to be in ability to express peace, harmony, forgiveness, and wisdom, he can still succeed in having a happy, prosperous home by establishing this Helper as the directive head of the home. This Helper will keep the home in balance by establishing peace, harmony, health, and happiness, as well as prosperity.

All you need to do to obtain the leadership of this successful Helper is to invite Him to take full charge, to turn the affairs of the family over to Him, and then follow His directions faithfully.

You have already guessed the name of this marvelous, loving helper. He is the Christ. When you choose Him for the head of your household, you cut your worries down to the minimum. All problems may be turned over to Him for solution, but everybody must cooperate with Him unselfishly and diligently in working out the details. A chair may be reserved for Him at the table and also in the living room. When He is remembered every hour of the day as being present, as listening to all conversations, every member of the family will be more careful of His words. Nagging, criticism, and gossip will drop out of style in the home. Goodwill and love will be the order of the household.

The father and mother will no longer need to worry about the affairs of such a home. Everything that would cause worry will be referred to the real head, and He will find a solution. All that the members of the family will need to do is to have faith in Him and to do their work well. He will preserve health in the home. He will prosper and bless all the members of the family. He will reveal the easy, happy way to meet neighborhood troubles. If the whole family can be induced to cooperate there will be no doubt about the establishment of perfect peace, harmony, and success in the home. However, if at first only one member of the family decides to serve the Christ, to the extent of his faith Christ will help, and He will do much for that home. The other members of the family will find it easy to cooperate more and more as time goes on.

Christ can be thought of as a person in the midst of your home even though as a matter of fact He really abides in the heart of each individual member. It helps the family to think of Him as being present in the household like a father possessing superlove and wisdom and giving a guiding hand and assuming the heavy responsibilities, while watching with keen interest the progress and welfare of the household. Christ can be personified as a member of the family and yet remain the true spiritual Self of each individual in the family. He is already present in everyone, but in order to become truly helpful in any household He must be invited, accepted, and obeyed. He is saying: "Lo, I am with you always, even unto the end of the world" and "My yoke is easy, and my burden is light."

Can you not hear Him speaking to your family in the words that He uttered through Jesus: "Follow me"? Can you not hear Him saying when strife shows its head: "Blessed are the merciful: for they shall obtain mercy," "Blessed are the peacemakers: for they shall be called sons of God," "Resist not him that is evil: but whosoever smiteth thee on thy right cheek, turn to him the other also," "For if ye love them that love you, what reward have ye?" "Ye therefore shall be perfect, as your heavenly Father is perfect," "Judge not, that ye be not judged," "And why beholdest thou the mote that is in thy brother's eye, but considerest not the beam that is in thine own eye?"

When wisdom is needed in the household, hear Him saying, "Ask, and it shall be given you; seek, and ye shall find; knock, and it shall be opened unto you."

When the family needs prosperity, hear these words: "Give, and it shall be given unto you: good measure, pressed down, shaken together, running over," "And all things, whatsoever ye shall ask in prayer, believing, ye shall receive," and "If ye shall ask anything in my name, that will I do."

When healing is needed you can hear Christ saying: "Go thy way; thy son liveth," "Daughter, be of good cheer; thy faith hath made thee whole," and "Fear not: only believe, and she shall be made whole."

For purity He speaks these words: "Already ye are clean because of the word which I have spoken unto you."

For gossip and criticism He says: "For by thy words thou shalt be justified, and by thy words thou shalt be condemned" and "And if a house be divided against itself, that house will not be able to stand."

In any emergency, who cannot hear Him speak thus: "According to your faith be it done unto you," "Be of good cheer; it is I; be not afraid," and "The things which are impossible with men are possible with God"?

And for food He speaks this wonderful word: "I am the bread of life."

These are only a few of His helpful words, but His presence in the home performs miracles.

Fifteen Sheets in the Wind

A complex thing is just a combination of simple things. A thousand years is a large accumulation of little minutes.

There are many complex problems to solve in the world today, but they are not so difficult when we realize that they are made up of simple things. We sometimes feel confused because there are so many new laws and rules to observe, so many extra duties to perform, and so many addresses to change, but everything is simplified when we reduce all these problems to a common denominator. There is one proved key to the solution of every

complex problem in life. God is the common denominator of every problem.

God is one God. He is not complex. Let God
help you now with your troubles. Meditate upon
the following thought as you place your whole problem in His hands:

*"There is but one Presence and one Power in my
life, God, who is unchanging love and power. There is
no other power to harm me."*

Because of the seeming complexities in the warring world, many people are becoming jittery. Of
course everyone has had to assume added responsibilities and do more work than usual, but it is not
work that tires us; it is our attitude toward our work
that wears us out. If a brake on your car drags, it
wastes your power and burns out your brake lining.

Worry is like a brake, but it is a useless brake. It
holds you back when you should be going ahead. If
you worry about the things that have to be done
instead of fearlessly and prayerfully doing them one
at a time you are burning up your brake linings.

The human mind is capable of doing much more
than it attempts, and human muscles have never
snapped from overwork on the part of the mind.

But in order to do more work the individual must
first bring his mind under the control of divine
order.

Divine order is based upon the truth that there is
but one power in the universe and that this power

is absolutely good. Perfect faith in this truth brings peace, order, and success into your life. Placing first things first is the initial step in putting your mind and your affairs in order. Give God first place in your heart and the other things in your life will fall into line. Establish yourself in the consciousness of unity with God and the complexities of life will begin to be untangled.

An experience told by a Unity teacher illustrates the practical application of this principle.

One day a woman's voice came to this teacher over the phone excitedly calling for prayers immediately. She explained that fifteen wet sheets had just been returned from the laundry, and they would have to be hung up on a line. She said she did not feel physically able to hang out all of those fifteen sheets, and she was discouraged and worn out.

The teacher then asked her how many sheets she was in the habit of hanging up at a time. The question puzzled the woman for a moment but she reluctantly answered: "One." So the teacher advised her to go ahead and hang up one sheet, realizing meanwhile that God was supplying her with the strength necessary to do it. When that was done, she was to take another sheet and hang it up in like manner. She was to go on from there with the other sheets, hanging up one sheet at a time as long as she was able. She was instructed to say this little prayer as she hung up each sheet: *"God is my help and my strength. Hanging up one sheet at a time is lots of fun, and it is easy too."*

The tired woman accepted the suggestion without much enthusiasm, but later on in the afternoon she called up the teacher and joyously reported that she had hung up the whole batch of sheets and was not the least bit tired. The teacher said: "You see, it was impossible for you to hang up fifteen sheets by sitting down and thinking how weak you were and how heavy the sheets were, but when you declared your inner strength and fearlessly tackled the job, you were able to do it. You proved the Power within you that enables you to proclaim: 'I can do all things through Christ which strengtheneth me.'"

This incident illustrates the great need in the world today for orderly thinking, which simply means considering one thing at a time, putting first things first. Disorderly thinking results when we try to carry all our burdens, real or imaginary, at one time. When we try to hang all of our sheets up at once, we become confused and depressed.

Divine order is established in our mind and affairs when we accept our unity with God. God is one, and one is the beginning of order. One is the common denominator of all problems in whole numbers. Therefore establish yourself in the consciousness of one, or unity, and do not let the many things of the world confuse you. Do one thing at a time. Do it well and rejoice in doing it.

Remember to free each problem with this decision: *"One thing, I do."* Praise God that you have abundant strength to accomplish this thing, and do not borrow trouble from your next duty. Jesus understood how suffering humanity overloads itself with borrowed burdens. His loving advice, if followed, would lessen by half the burdens of humanity. Here it is: "Sufficient unto the day is the evil thereof." This is Jesus' way of saying, "One thing at a time." Jesus was more than an idealist; He was interested in the solution of everyday problems.

Remember that you can simplify the multiplicity of things you worry about having to do by finding within yourself the consciousness of divine order, which is the presence of the one God. You will save time and conserve your energy if you will begin today to realize that there is but one Presence and one Power in your life, and that that Presence and Power is good, and is always with you.

Life's problems are made easy when our mind and muscles work in harmony with God, but we waste our energy when we worry about complex things. There are no complexities in Spirit. Truth is simple; your work is simple. Everything is simple when you do one thing at a time under God's direction.

People who worry are following many gods: the god of money, the god of personal egotism, the god of pleasure, the god of worry, and the little gods of doubt and fear.

God's desire always has been that His children be happy, but this happiness is possible to them only when they accept His plan by following His commandments in Spirit and in Truth.

The first great commandment has to do with God as the unit from which all things spring. In the "one God" we find the solution to all of our problems. God represents unity, and when man seeks unity with God, he discovers that divine order and harmony are pervading every detail of his life. Jesus called attention to the importance of unity of purpose in the words "The first [commandment] is, Hear, O Israel; The Lord our God, the Lord is one: and thou shalt love the Lord thy God with all thy heart, and with all thy soul, and with all thy mind, and with all thy strength."

How to Overcome the Jitters

During these trying times we need to cultivate the spiritual strength and poise that God has given us.

There is a subtle hidden power within every one of us that is ready and waiting to come forth and lead us on to victory. It responds to the call of our faith.

When the affairs of our world seem to be tangled and we do not know how to untangle them, then it is time for us to draw upon our inner spiritual source of power and to cut the snarl fearlessly, as

Alexander the Great cut the Gordian knot with his sword.

Listen, troubled soul, to the voice of the Spirit of Truth within you, and it will bring you wisdom from God according to the promise of Jesus. "When he, the Spirit of truth, is come, he shall guide you into all the truth." Now please sit quietly where you will not be disturbed and realize that in Spirit you are a child of God. Remember that He is your loving Father and that He desires you to be happy, healthy, wise, and successful.

When you insist on having your own way and refuse to let God's perfect will lead you, you interfere with His plan to help you. Therefore if you wish to get your personal will out of the way, repeat this statement twelve times silently and slowly:

"Lord, not my will, but thine, be done."

Remember that there is but one Power in the universe, and it is good, because it is God power. Now repeat the following statement twelve times:

"I am not afraid to deliver my will and all of my worldly affairs to God so that His will may control them." Repeat also:

"I now set aside my personal likes and dislikes, my pride and grievances. I know that the power of God active in me is bringing my own to me under the divine law. There is nothing to fear, for God's will is good will. Though all the world be in confusion, there

is peace within me, for God is directing my affairs, leading me beside the still waters, and restoring my soul.

"No matter what has been said or done, no evil can come near me. The rod or will of my Father will bring good out of every dark experience. I am not afraid of things to come nor of rumors of hardships to face. I know that God is caring for His children wherever they may be. Because I have set my love upon Him, He will deliver me. Through my faith in Him I am helping to bring His kingdom onto the earth.

"God in me greets God in everybody I meet. I am one with God through Christ, who is the Son of God abiding in me. There can be no confusion in my life or in my body, for Christ is directing my affairs and harmonizing my body functions. I am being renewed daily by the life of Christ. I am no longer under the law of sin and death; I am a new creature in Christ.

"God gives me wisdom to solve my every problem. Each day's difficulties are transformed by God's loving guidance into stepping-stones on which I may rise to find more good things. I am no longer afraid of what will happen tomorrow, for I have given tomorrow to God. Peace reigns in my body and my affairs. God is in His heaven within me, and all is right in my world."

Why Did You Do It?

We are usually guided in our actions by our mental attitude. Sometimes we act unwisely because our reasoning is upset by fear, while at other times we are able to act wisely because our mind is poised in an attitude of love and goodwill.

No doubt many people who do wrong are driven to it by fear. A man may steal because he is afraid he will not have enough money to meet his needs. A man may murder another man because he is afraid the man will harm him or cause him trouble. Wars are sometimes caused by ungrounded fears between nations. When Herod, the Roman ruler, heard of Jesus' birth in Bethlehem and was told that Jesus was to become the king of the Jews, he was afraid he would lose his power as a ruler. Because of this fear he ordered his men to kill all the male children in Bethlehem that were two years old and under in a vain attempt to destroy Jesus.

Some persons join a church because they are afraid they will receive punishment after death if they do not. Others join a church because they love God and are happy in His service. Children often lie to their parents because they are afraid they will be punished if they tell the truth. Some drivers obey the traffic laws because they are afraid of punishment, while others obey the laws because they love and respect other drivers and want to cooperate with them.

God is love, and love is always cooperative and constructive. Doing something right and good because we love truth and goodness helps us to be strong, courageous, dependable, and happy. Fear is a negative power that really exists only in the mind of the one who is afraid. It is caused by a lack of confidence in the power of love. Fear is like darkness, and love is like light. Darkness is nothing but the absence of light, and fear is the absence of love in a person's heart. When we are in physical darkness, even the light of a little candle will help us to find our way. Darkness has no power to put out the light of that candle, but there is power in the light of the candle to dispel the darkness.

So it is with love and fear. Fear has no power to destroy love, but perfect love can cast out fear. Fear is a mental state of darkness, while love is a mental state of light. We fear something that we think may come in the future, such as failure, poverty, sickness, or the punishment we are told may come after death; but we must remember that this fear exists only in our mind. Job said: "The thing which I fear cometh upon me."

God's love is so real and so powerful that we also become powerful when we express His love in all our thoughts, words, and actions. When God's love abides in us, we cannot be frightened into doing that which is evil. The light of love casts the darkness of fear from our mind, revealing to us the good in the thing that we feared.

We often fear things because we do not understand them, but love gives us courage to look for and understand the good things that are all about us. Love helps us to understand our neighbors better. If they appear to be unfriendly, we can, by the light of love, discover the good that is in them instead of fearing them. Sometimes, however, when we refuse to let God's love help us, we cannot find that good. But there is always good in everyone, because God put it there.

The Psalms can help us to find our inner courage. Here are some words from the Twenty-third Psalm that will help us: "I will fear no evil; for thou art with me." If we repeat these words a number of times silently, we awaken courage in our soul. By repeating such words of Truth we assure ourselves of the omnipresence of God's love. In this assurance we find courage to march on through even "the valley of the shadow of death" without fear.

If David had been afraid of Goliath he would never have faced him; but David had courage to meet and overcome the giant because he loved God. Because love, like light, is real, it overcomes fear, for the power of fear is as unreal as the power of darkness.

When you ask yourself, "Why did I do this unwise

thing?" ask yourself also if fear prompted you to do it. If you did something unwise because you were afraid, you should begin at once, through the power of love, to cast fear from your consciousness. You can cultivate love by first forgiving yourself and then loving God with all your heart, soul, mind, and strength, and your neighbor as yourself.

With love in your heart, you will not need to be a slave to fear in the future. You will do what is right because you will not be afraid. When you are one with God's love, no fearful thought will be able to cause you to do what is wrong. Neither can fear cause you to be sick when certain symptoms of sickness are called to your attention. God's love and life are greater than any of these false appearances, and God's power will protect you as you stand firmly with Him. Jesus promised: "All things are possible to him that believeth."

Let us therefore stand firmly with God and believe that His love and righteousness and healing power are greater than all the fears, doubts, and troubles of the world. When we remember that we are children of the living God and practice loving Him more than we fear things, we shall find that we are standing in God's love and that we are permeated with and infolded in His healing, life-giving, courage-giving power. We shall be able to stand still and see the salvation of the Lord as the fearful waters of our troubled Red Sea are parted for us to go safely through them.

The Right Answer

The right answer to any problem can be reached only when God's perfect principles are applied. To get the right answer in solving a mathematical problem, the correct principles of mathematics must be used.

God's principles, used correctly by His children, will solve all their worldly problems. One of the principles in mathematics is that two and two always equals four. In the use of God's principles, we may say that love and understanding, when used rightly, always equal success.

The Christ way is the right way, because it involves the right use of God's principles and not the ignorant use of man's emotions. Jesus Christ said: "I am the way, and the truth, and the life." He also said: "I am the light of the world."

When God created all things in the beginning, He pronounced all of them good. Therefore goodness is one of the sustaining principles that permeate all of His creations. When we rightly use the principles of divine goodness, we shall not fail. Therefore, when making a decision, we must be sure that the principles of divine goodness enter into our decision. If we will follow it, the Christ light will reveal to us a way in which God's wonderful principles of love and goodness, peace and unity, can be used to bring us the right solution to our problems.

When we are faced with a problem, we are often moved by our personal will to do something drastic that is not in harmony with God's divine principles. When we do this drastic thing, we cannot get the right answer. When we are afraid to try to decide what our answer shall be, we are not using God's principles; we need to drop our fear and put in its place our faith in God's principles to take care of the whole matter.

When we put our problem into God's loving hands and stop worrying about it, the Christ light will show us the way to cooperate with God's principles in obtaining the right answer.

We should never let hate, fear, jealousy, worry, and selfishness influence us in arriving at a decision. These negative ideas are man's creations and not God's; they are not in accord with God's good principles and will therefore give us the wrong answer. That which is true will endure forever, but that which is not true, while it may seem to last for a time, will fade away under the light of God's Truth.

If we put all of our problems into God's hands and let His will be done through us, instead of our following our own will, we shall no longer need to worry, for our problem will either disappear entirely or God will help us to solve it in just the right way. With God's help, other persons who are involved in our problem may change their attitude and cooperate with us in seeking a better understanding of our problem.

When we have faith in them, God's principles will show us new and helpful ways to solve our problems. God's principles will never cause us to fight evil, for when we fight evil, we are unwisely adding our own thoughts of discord to our problem instead of erasing it by letting the light of Truth shine upon it.

When we learn to put all our problems into God's hands, we shall be saved from many heart-aches and bodily ills. When we stop worrying and being anxious, we shall relax and so open the way for nature's perfect plan of the renewal of our organism to work freely and joyously in us. Therefore, when we put our problem into God's hands, His healing power can work more freely in our body and our affairs.

**There is but one Presence
and one Power here.**

A Prayer Drill

First Day. *There is but one Presence and one Power in my life, God, who is unchanging love and power. There can be no other power to harm me.*

Second Day. *Because God is one, He makes all complicated things in my affairs simple and easy to understand.*

Third Day. *God is my help in every need. He helps me to keep my affairs in divine order by showing me how to do first things first.*

Fourth Day. *I can do all things through Christ, the Son of God dwelling in me.*

Fifth Day. *Divine order is being established in my mind and affairs because I am cultivating perfect faith in the one supreme power of God as the only power in my life.*

Sixth Day. *This one thing, I do in the name of God's Christ within me.*

Seventh Day. *I love God, the only Presence and Power in the universe, with all my heart, with all my soul, with all my mind, and with all my strength.*

Chapter 9

Living the Full Life

Life is now and God is eternally with me.

Live Today

TODAY is eternal. The present is the only time in which we can do anything. We cannot do anything yesterday or tomorrow; but we can brood over the things that have happened in the past or worry about the things that may happen in the future and waste our wonderful today.

The wisest thing we can do is to live today and enjoy life now. Today is always here and is the only time we can actually do anything. The past is gone, and it can live only in our memory. Longfellow, in his "A Psalm of Life," gives us a good thought on this subject. He writes:

> "Trust no Future, howe'er pleasant!
> Let the dead Past bury its dead!
> Act, act in the living present!
> Heart within, and God o'erhead!"

Our thoughts today are like seed, and we may be harvesting today the fruit of our thoughts of yesterday. If they were good thoughts, we can rejoice in their good fruit; but if our seed thoughts were negative and unhappy ones, we should be careful not to eat of their fruit by spending our time worrying about the negation and unhappiness. Instead of finding fault with the bad fruit, we should today be planting seed thoughts that will bear good fruit so that when tomorrow arrives and becomes today, we can rejoice.

God is with us today. We should enjoy His good presence instead of crying over the mistakes that we or others have made in the past. The past can live today only in our memory of it. Therefore, let us use our memory joyfully.

It is well to remember the good things of the past, but we should also give thanks for the good things of the present. We cannot improve the future by worrying about it, and when we worry, we are wasting today. Let us enjoy today and live it fully.

God can help us to live each day fully if we will become aware of His presence in Spirit and in Truth and work with Him to do His will in all that we think, say, and do. If there are things that happened in the past that we do not seem to be able to forget, let us fill our mind so full of the love that God has given us to express today that we forget the mistakes of the past.

We can cast off the heavy burdens of unpleasant

memories of the past by forgiving those who we think mistreated us and by also forgiving our own mistakes of the past. Today is a new day. Today is a time in which we should rejoice. If we rejoice in today's beauty and blessings, we shall also rejoice when tomorrow becomes today.

God is with us today, and He is always here. There is no such thing as time in infinite Mind, for it is everywhere present forever. The Christ in Jesus explained this when He said: "Before Abraham was born, I am." He did not say: "Before Abraham was born, I was born," but He said, "I am," showing that He realized that God's idea of His Son is now present and is eternal.

So when we say, "I am a child of God," we are speaking the Truth about God's idea of His Son in us. As we realize this Truth, the things that are unlike God's good creation will disappear from our mind, and we shall live joyously in the presence of our Father-God.

This present moment is our opportunity to express the wonderful gifts that God has given us. When we do not rejoice in His goodness but, instead, spend our time worrying and being unhappy about the past and the future, we are not living, in the true sense of the word.

God is our life, so let us at this moment try to measure up to the fullness of that life. God has made all things good, and because He made us, we

are therefore good. We can demonstrate that goodness by believing in it and by thinking God's
thoughts with Him now.

We must not put off our good until tomorrow
nor put off our troubles until tomorrow. Troubles
are nothing in the sight of God; therefore, we can
cast our burdens, or troubles, upon the Lord and
they will be nothing to us.

Let us realize that today is a new beginning, that
old things have passed away, and that we are truly
children of the living God. As we rejoice and give
thanks for God's goodness, we are able to feel and
to make His goodness active in us at this present
moment.

"Now is the acceptable time." God is with us
now, and the kingdom of heaven is at hand. Jesus
said: "The kingdom of God is within you." Spending
the present time in seeking the kingdom of God
within us and doing the will of God is the most
acceptable and happy way to use our unending present moment.

Use Your Energy Wisely

Our Father-God gives us freely of His energy
because He wants us to use this energy to grow in
our understanding of His perfect creation that is all
about us, so that we can become living manifestations on earth of His perfect idea of man in heaven.

He created man in the beginning as an idea of a Son who is like His Maker in Spirit and Truth.

It is our Father-God's desire that all men become beings who, of their own choice, will bring into manifestation in their bodies His perfect idea of His Son. Our heavenly Father wants us to become His children who understand Him in Spirit and to enjoy His good creation as we become channels for the manifestation in the world of His perfect ideas.

Adam was the first man who was given a physical body, and he was placed in a garden where he could become a child of God and be his Father's helper in activity and in understanding. But this first man failed to understand the true goodness of his Father-God and chose to believe in evil as well as good. Therefore, he could no longer enjoy the beautiful garden. He began to use his energy in ways that were negative and destructive, and to learn by hard experiences that he is a child of God.

Of course the story of Adam is only an allegory to explain how God's idea of man became a manifest individual. During the countless years since Adam's time, man has made many mistakes; but he is on his way to the attainment of a better understanding of his spiritual relationship to his heavenly Father. In order to help His children to understand how they can become aware that they are His perfect children living in physical bodies, He sent Jesus Christ into the world to be an example of how everyone may become His perfect Son made manifest in the world. Christ is God's perfect-man idea, created in the beginning. Jesus was the son of man, but He was also a manifestation of God's Son living in the world of the Adam man, the world of materiality.

Jesus Christ is therefore the Way-Shower to help all people find God's perfect idea of who they truly are in spirit and truth. Jesus Christ has pointed the way for us, which is also the Truth and the life that the heavenly Father has planned for all His children. We are all on our way to becoming perfect children of God and joint heirs with Jesus Christ.

Jesus taught us to use our God-given energy constructively by always expressing our Father's goodwill in our thoughts, words, and acts. Jesus told us not to be angry with those who offend us but to overcome their anger with love, peace, and joy.

In the Lord's Prayer, Jesus Christ is showing us how to work with our Father to bring His good creation into our world. "Thy kingdom come. Thy will be done, as in heaven, so on earth." By affirming these words, and letting them become active in our mind and body, Jesus Christ has shown us how we can use our energy to establish our unity with our Father in Spirit and thereby abide with Him in the kingdom of heaven, which is now at hand on the earth. Jesus told us that the kingdom of heaven is with us; that is, it is potentially within us and can become manifest on the earth through our faith. We must discover God's kingdom by lifting our own understanding to the place where we can see that the kingdom of heaven is indeed at hand and that it is within us in Spirit.

It is possible for one man to dwell in the kingdom of heaven while his next-door neighbor may dwell in a state of discord and unhappiness and be dominated by the cares of the world. Jesus taught us that we can overcome the cares of the world by using our faith in our Father's love and goodness to behold and enjoy the good things that he has made for us.

God made everything good, but we cannot bring that goodness into our world by fighting the things of the world that appear to be evil. We must not waste our energy by using it to fight evil. We must overcome evil with good. When we are pessimistic, unhappy, angry, or dissatisfied, we should realize that we are wasting our God-given energy; we should therefore stop, and begin using our God-given energy to build up our understanding of righteousness and Truth.

Jesus has taught us to seek only that which is good, and so lift our vision above evil. We can begin today to practice using our energy in thinking, speaking, and doing only that which is good, loving, kind, wise, and joyful. Sad thoughts are not constructive thoughts, but joyous thoughts produce good results. We can live in a joyous world right where we are if we will use our energy to the glory of God. Such use of our energy will bring harmony into our home, more joy into our social affairs, and also add efficiency, pleasure, and love to the work we are doing.

We must learn that forgiveness is more effective in bringing our good to us than condemnation and ill will. Peace and goodwill can overcome that which does not seem to be good. When we use our energy in the wrong way, we often destroy the health of our bodies. Worry, fear, and discord tear down the cells of our body, while love, forgiveness, and harmony help to build up the health of our body. So it is in our association with other people, in our prosperity, and in every phase of our life: if we use God's way, which is the loving, peaceful, harmonious way, we shall bring good into our affairs and we shall find a new joy in living.

Giving thanks and praising are wonderful ways to use our energy constructively.

As we praise God and our fellow men we can realize that Jesus Christ is with us, helping us to become perfect children of God. As we help ourselves and others to use our energy in good thinking, constructive speaking, and friendly acts, we help to bring peace on earth and goodwill to men. The day is coming when all men will be aware of their unity with God through Christ. Let us today lift ourselves up to a place in God consciousness so that the ills of the flesh can no longer torment us. When we realize our unity with Christ, we are growing up to be perfect children of God. Therefore, let us never waste our energy in negative thinking such as criticism, fear, worry, anger, ill will.

Let us use our energy to be joyous, thankful, loving, and harmonious. Let us follow the Christ way every day, and so find the joy of living and be freed from the negations of the world.

How to Relax

Your physical body is made up of millions of little parts called cells. These little fellows are intelligent, and they are busy doing things for your good.

You do not know these little cells very well, even though they are very close to you. You would find them very interesting entities if you could know every one of them individually. But since there are so many of them, to know them all would be like knowing everybody in the world.

Since you cannot know all these cells individually, there is a way in which you can appeal to their intelligence, for they are your servants. They are your faithful subjects, although you do not direct their activities individually. You have efficient assistants who pass your orders on to the multitude of cells.

You are like a mighty king upon whom millions

are depending for their inspiration and their very existence.

These little cells make up the various parts and function-centers of your body. Some form your head; some, your hands; some, your feet; one group forms your stomach, and still another group forms your lungs.

There are brain centers in different parts of your body that are directing the activities of the function-centers under their control. These brain centers are like broadcasting stations; they are constantly sending messages through the nervous system and also through other means to all the cells in their localities. These brain centers receive messages from the subconscious mind, which, in turn, receives instructions from the conscious mind. The brain centers are like a chain of broadcasting stations, which take up a program from headquarters and distribute it in their respective localities.

Your subconscious mind controls these centers for you, thus carrying on a vast and intricate work. If you did not have this faithful assistant and if you had to think of drawing in the air each time you breathed, you would be so busy with supervising your breathing that you could not do much else, and while you were busy directing your breathing, your heart might stop beating. However, the faithful subconscious mind and the brain centers relieve you of all this detail work and faithfully perform these operations and many others for you, including the renewing of injured parts, the growing of fingernails and hair, the digesting of food, and the circulating of the blood, which keeps the interior of the body clean and in order.

The subconscious mind had its original instructions from the Creator, to the effect that the body was to be kept in perfect running order and that all its functions were to remain harmonious and healthy. The subconscious mind has tried to follow these divine instructions, and will do so except when you direct it otherwise.

Your conscious mind dominates your subconscious mind. You can tell your subconscious mind the Truth, or you can tell it error. It is very obedient and it will carry your instructions on to the brain centers and to the cells.

One of the most unfortunate error messages that you can give to your subconscious mind to pass on to your body-cell people is a decree of condemnation. You may condemn some person outside, but your subconscious mind inside is impressed with the condemnation idea and carries it into your body, where it plays havoc among your cell people. Condemnation snarls them up, stops their free and natural functioning, and makes them very unhappy. Such thoughts as fear, unhappiness, and hate also affect the cell people of your body adversely.

When your little cells receive the broadcast message of condemnation, their free expression is hindered. They become inharmonious, and when a large group of cells in a certain locality are continually commanded to resist or to become tense, you develop a chronic ailment.

We sleep in order to relax, but sometimes we do not sleep and so do not relax. The reason we do not relax is that some destructive or unpleasant message has disturbed our body-cell community.

The idea of condemnation often holds our body nation in bondage. Forgiveness is one of the most important messages that you can broadcast to your cells. When you lie down at night to go to sleep, forgive everybody and everything. Send everyone thoughts of love and good will. As you forgive, a harmonious message will at the same time be broadcast in your body, and there will be an unloosing and a freeing of your functions. The little cells that were before inactive or on a strike will respond to your message of love and go joyously back to work. The blood and lymph will circulate freely through your organs again, and you will rest while your bodily conditions will have an opportunity to improve.

You are the one who has full charge of the broadcasting programs that are being sent to your body-cell people. You have, in fact, a monopoly of the broadcasting business in your realm. Therefore, if your cells are not getting the right kind of instructions, no one but yourself is to blame.

You can open your broadcasting station to the Christ or superconscious mind. The Christ will "put on a program" for you that will thrill and revive your cell subjects.

You must first forgive everybody and everything in order that the Christ mind may bless your body with its healing life. Your cells must be set free by forgiveness before they can relax and receive the great message.

You are a mighty monarch ruling over a populous domain, and you have at your disposal a wonderful system for broadcasting to every member of that domain.

As you make your cells happy, they, in turn, make you happy; therefore, be good to your body-cell people. Be a wise and loving ruler and broadcaster.

Frustrating Frustration

A man's nature is so ordered that he must have faith in something. He should choose this something wisely, because if it later fails him, he is likely to become very much upset.

Men sometimes choose unworthy things to put their faith in. They choose a person, a piece of ground, an organization, a monarch, a political party, a career, or maybe just a rabbit's foot. When later they find that their choice was wrong, and the thing they put their faith in was undependable or unworthy, they become terribly disappointed.

A person may also become disappointed when certain little things that he counted on are taken away from him, or when something he has been doing does not turn out in the way he had planned. When disappointed he may easily become discouraged, or he may try to save face by putting on an act to cover up the disappointment he feels.

It is good for everyone to have something stable and unchanging to pin his faith to. If we place our faith in God, we shall never be sorry we did so. Those who lift their faith to the high level of God's infinite love, wisdom, and power will seldom know frustration even if disappointments do come into their lives.

Great peace abides with a person who places his faith in God. Such a faith can soften a shock that would crush the average man. Those who have not placed their faith in the Almighty find that they must do something with it, and they therefore place too much dependence in the lesser things, in worldly things. These lesser, worldly things may seem to be adequate for a time, but someday they are likely to fail under some great strain.

When a person finds that his earthly ideal tumbles—because it has feet of clay—he realizes that he has reached a turning point in his life. At such a time he may turn back or go forward. He may become discouraged and turn off the good road into bypaths of crime, dissipation, or bitterness. On the other hand, he may move forward with a renewed spirit to win.

It is said that man's extremity is God's opportunity, and a disappointment that shakes his faith in the old ideal may cause him to turn to God and establish his faith in a power that cannot fail. If after that something should go wrong with his plans, he will realize that since God cannot fail, it is he himself who has failed because he did not work with God's perfect law. Therefore he will seek divine guidance so that he can overcome this failure. His inner strength then becomes greater than any obstacle, because it is established in an all-powerful God.

Perhaps we feel frustrated when one of our plans fails, and then our first impulse may be to be angry, bitter, or resentful, or to feel sorry for ourselves. This may lead us to complain and to use bitter or profane words. This is very poor practice at such a time, because it makes things worse instead of better.

When anything goes wrong, we must be ready to do something helpful instead of adding to the damage already done. Negative words, cursing, and grumbling are weak and worse than useless in getting us out of trouble. On the other hand, constructive words are strong and helpful at such times.

Truth students have found that every person has at his disposal a means that he can use to turn defeat into victory and to transform his life and his affairs. This means is the use of affirmations of Truth. No greater physical effort is required in making a miracle-working affirmation of Truth than is used in foolish swearing or grumbling. When you make an affirmation of Truth, you set in motion the constructive forces of God's law.

Cursing, speaking angry words, whining, and crying only add to your confusion. Therefore turn your word power into affirmations of Truth and back these up by your faith in God. Thus armed, you will be able to overcome every adversity and to preserve your spiritual poise. Affirmations of Truth will aid you in operating in more perfect accord with the constructive laws of God, which are designed to promote our welfare.

Remember that your words are like seed. When you speak a word, you plant it, and God gives the increase.

When you speak words of doubt, fear, and anger, you are planting seeds that will bear, after their kind, the fruits of doubt, fear, and anger. When you affirm the Truth about God's goodness and love, when you bless the Christ in others, you are planting seed that will bear a wondrous harvest of goodness and love, after their kind.

Would you reap happiness, prosperity, and good health? Then plant words of happiness, prosperity, and good health and stop talking about your troubles. By planting seeds of Truth, you will be able to nullify and render powerless the negative words that, if indulged in, will produce a harvest of frustration.

God's words are more powerful than negative words. By speaking God's words, you can avoid frustration.

If something unpleasant occurs, instead of thinking of it as evil, why not plant a good thought in your mind by using an affirmation of Truth, and let it produce something good for you in the future? When last year's troublesome weeds decay, they can be made to enrich the soil that will bear better fruit for you when you plant good seeds in it.

In like manner the residue of your unhappy experiences can be made to contribute to a better yield of happiness and success in the present time if you plant good word seed this time. Affirmations that declare the Truth about God and your relationship to Him will always produce a rich harvest of health, happiness, and prosperity for you.

Rising Out of the "Dumps"

The "dumps" are a state of mind. When a few conditions seem to be unfavorable and you react negatively by being worried or fearful, you find yourself in the dumps. As a matter of fact, the dumps are in you, not you in them.

God does not wish you to suffer, to be afraid, or to be in the dumps. God is perfect love. Perfect love casts out all fear. Perfect love supplies your every need. God has provided all the good that you need, before you ask for it. You must have faith in God's good before you can discover it and use it. Go into your "inner chamber" and shut the door and ask of the Father in secret, and He will reward you openly. This is what Jesus Christ promised.

Put out of your mind all worry thoughts and ask in faith. You do not have faith when you worry. Prove your faith by giving thanks. Rejoice and be glad. Thank God with a glad heart that your prayer is answered. Believe that it has been answered, and rejoice. Express more love.

You are God's child: you are as dear to God as the prodigal son was to his father. When he returned, his father met him with open arms and he shared in all the good things that the father had. How do we return to our Father's house? By taking our attention away from malice, jealousy, greed, lust, fear, and doubt, and turning it in love toward our Father, God. "God is no respecter of persons," but the individual must choose whether he will cooperate with God fully or follow his own selfish inclination by going "into a far country." When he chooses the selfish way and reaps unsatisfactory results, he may feel that God does not love him. The selfish way includes doubt and fear as well as greed and pride.

We must be obedient to the law of good. If we expect good, we shall receive good. We cannot enjoy the good unless we are obedient to the laws of good. Every person really wants only good, but some persons think that good is uninteresting, not understanding that their very desire for unworthy things is but a misdirected yearning after the good. They do not understand their desires. They will never be satisfied with anything less than good. Husks may appear attractive, but husks cannot satisfy soul hunger. We must learn to give thanks for our good now. If we wait for the good to manifest, we put off the day of our thanksgiving, and it may never come. It is therefore very important that we learn how to be thankful, and that we also employ much of our time in expressing thankfulness and in rejoicing because of the fundamental truth that God has already answered our prayers.

When we really feel the joy of thanksgiving, then do we prove that we have faith. It is absolutely necessary for us to have faith if our prayers are to be answered. Faith is that something which reaches out into the invisible and takes hold of the good that God has already prepared for us in Spirit, and makes it tangible for us. Let us learn to rejoice. Let our rejoicing have its roots in a consciousness that God is more important than anything else in the whole universe. All things are dependent upon God, and by being thankful to God we put ourselves in touch with the original Source of every good thing.

Let us meditate upon some of the promises from the Bible that concern rejoicing. As we read these, let us catch the spirit of joy that they radiate, realizing that our prayers are already answered. We should push aside every doubt and fear, and let the joy of the Lord enter our hearts.

"Thou shalt rejoice before Jehovah thy God in all that thou puttest thy hand unto."

> "Let all those that take refuge in
>   thee rejoice,
> Let them ever shout for joy,
>   because thou defendest them:
> Let them also that love thy name
>   be joyful in thee."

> "Thou hast turned for me my
>   mourning into dancing;
> Thou hast loosed my sackcloth,
>   and girded me with gladness."

> "Let the righteous be glad; let
>   them exult before God:

> Yea, let them rejoice with
> gladness."

> "These things have I spoken unto
> you, that my joy may be in you,
> and *that* your joy may be made
> full."

> "The fruit of the Spirit is love, joy,
> peace."

"Rejoice in the Lord always: again I will say, Rejoice. Let your forbearance be known unto all men. The Lord is at hand. In nothing be anxious; but in everything by prayer and supplication with thanksgiving let your requests be made known unto God. And the peace of God, which passeth all understanding, shall guard your hearts and your thoughts in Christ Jesus."

Some thoughts are stored away so deep in the subconscious mind that they never come to the notice of the conscious mind, yet they are producing effects upon your life and happiness. A thought of hate may become subconscious, and while the conscious mind may not feel it, the emotion may work out in some bodily ailment. The object of hate may have been forgotten by the conscious mind, but the subconscious remembers, and if not looked after, goes on hating until it destroys the body.

When you stop to realize that every thought that has ever been in your mind has left its living record in your consciousness, you will understand why you should be very careful in selecting your daily thoughts. Good, harmonious, pure, loving, living thoughts take up their abode in the subconscious as veritable angels that fill the body with health and happiness.

Why Pray?

Prayer changes things in our life by first changing our attitude toward God. We pray to God because we know that He is the Giver of our very life and all things that we need.

Prayer is a means of becoming more definitely associated with God's love, substance, harmony, wisdom, and power. God is omnipresent, and by praying we become more aware of His presence. As we pray we bring our thoughts and words more definitely into accord with the power of God's Word.

All things were made by His Word, and these things bear His spiritual mark of perfection. Sometimes we see the manifestation of God's good works as "in a mirror, darkly," because we do not understand the wonder and harmony of His perfect plan. We therefore do not always appreciate His perfect works and cooperate with Him as we would if we could see as He sees.

Through prayer we learn to see all things in a better light. True prayer does not consist in begging God for things we want, because God has already given us everything we need and He is more willing to give than we are to receive. True prayer is actually a way of getting better acquainted with God and His love. Many people lift their eyes toward the sky when they pray, not because they feel God exists only in the sky, but because lifting their eyes symbolizes the turning of their attention away from worldly thoughts and feelings toward a higher spiritual understanding of their relationship to Him.

As we gain a better understanding of God, the spiritual source of all things, we are able to accept His rich gifts more freely. God must be worshiped in spirit and in truth. You remember that Jesus told the woman at the well that God must be worshiped in Spirit and in Truth. We worship God in Truth when we speak the Truth about His creation, which includes our body, our affairs, and our friends. We worship God in Truth when we speak the Truth about His good creation and we worship Him in Spirit when we put all our selfish thoughts out of mind and speak to Him with our whole being in loving devotion. We must speak to Him with sincerity and love from the true Self within us. In this way we attune our consciousness to God's loving presence.

We speak affirmations of Truth to build up our faith in God's power. When we affirm: "With God all things are possible" over and over again, we increase our awareness of His mighty, omnipresent power. Our affirmations of Truth bring our minds into God's way so that all our thoughts and words come into harmony with His good plan.

True prayer lifts our mind into a state of unity with the great Mind that controls the universe. We each have a subconscious mind that is obedient to the instructions given it by our conscious thoughts and words. Our subconscious mind takes care of the functions of our body. When we keep saying or thinking, "I am sick," or "I am weak," we instruct our subconscious mind to establish these negative conditions in our body. This procedure is not according to God's good wishes for our welfare. But the subconscious mind also obeys us when we speak the Truth to it. When we say, "I am well; I am strong," the subconscious mind at once gets busy and works for health and strength.

Often, after we have made a few true affirmations, we lapse into negation and begin to think and speak about our sickness or weakness, and when we do this our subconscious mind receives a greater number of negative suggestions than positive suggestions. Therefore, if we would give proper authority to our subconscious mind so that it can work constructively and in harmony with God's good plan, we must be faithful and persistent in speaking Truth every day and many times a day.

Many children have learned "The Prayer of Faith," the first line of which is "God is my help in every need," and they repeat it often. This simple little prayer has worked wonders for the children by bringing them closer consciously and subconsciously to a realization of God's omnipresent power and goodness.

An effective prayer is an affirmation of Truth concerning God's perfect creation. An affirmation spoken faithfully, either audibly or silently, changes our way of thinking from negative, selfish thoughts to positive, Godlike thoughts. When we speak to God in His own language of Truth and Spirit, He helps us to find and to use the abundant blessings that He has prepared for us. Divine order can be established in our body and affairs only as we let God thoughts govern our way of thinking.

People who do not pray allow their minds to wander into all kinds of scattered, negative ways of thinking. Prayer helps us to bring divine order into our lives, which results in a greater degree of health, happiness, and prosperity for us.

Let us pray constantly in Spirit and in Truth by using good thoughts that will keep our life in tune with God's plan. By prayer we bring our thoughts

into the kingdom of heaven where we find wisdom, harmony, peace, health, prosperity.

Obedience to God helps us to enjoy His glory. So
let us pray with faith that God's will is now being
done on our earth, in our body, and in all our
affairs as it is being done in heaven. Jesus gave us
this teaching in the Lord's Prayer. Whenever we
repeat this prayer, let us enter into its spirit so that
we may become unified with God's consciousness
of loving power and glory.

Life is now and God is eternally with me.

A Prayer Drill

First Day. *I am always harmonious, happy, prosperous, and healthy, because I live, move, and have my being in God.*

Second Day. *Because I have placed my faith in God I am poised and unafraid. He is showing me how to proceed.*

Third Day. *Because God is more important to me than anything in the whole world, nothing can disturb me or make me afraid. Seeing God in all things makes them more beautiful and helpful.*

Fourth Day. *I have nothing to fear, for God is here.*

Fifth day. *To this problem before me I say: "God bless you that you may become a blessing to me and to all."*

Sixth Day. *I plant good words wherever I go, and God gives me a rich increase of good things.*

Seventh Day. *My words are Spirit, and they are life, and they shall not return unto me void, but shall accomplish that whereunto they are sent.*

Chapter 10

God Is Greater Than Our Fears

**I am still in the silence of my mind
and I am at peace.**

Just a Minute

NO minute spent with God in prayer is ever wasted. Just one minute with God can bring you more good than many hours spent alone in struggling with your worldly problems.

Man measures time by seconds, minutes, hours, days, months, years, and centuries, but God's time is always now, even though man may try to divide time into todays, yesterdays, and tomorrows. God is always with you, now, this very minute.

One minute spent with God brings you joy, peace, harmony, and well-being. When you are with God, you are free from the regrets of the past and the fears for the future. You can, if you choose, abide now, this minute, in the wondrous power of God's unchanging love and guidance.

This present minute lived with God can free you from the burdens of past memories and the dread of the future, for now is the acceptable time in which you can enjoy a visit with God. All is right with God this minute. Why not tune in for a visit with Him and enjoy His eternal love? If the hours of your day are dragging along in a weary procession as you groan under the burdens of memories of past mistakes, old grudges, and unforgiveness, just take a minute to cast your burdens on the Lord. Or, if you are burdened by worries about and fear of what may happen in the future, take a minute with God to find the right path into a pleasant future. In this minute relax and feel the freedom from all past and future problems as you abide now in God's eternal, unchanging goodness.

If you have had a long, hard day and are worn out, and you are concerned about what will happen tomorrow, and you are doubting that you will be able to meet its problems, why not relax and take a little period of rest as you say to your troubles: "Just a minute, please, while I speak to the Master of my life and let Him show me what is best for me to do to solve my problems according to His love and wisdom." Then seek God with your whole heart as you listen to His still small voice. Feel the power of His word as He speaks silently: "Peace, be still" or "Be still, and know that I am God." Rest in His assurance, and you will be strengthened and guided.

Whenever anything comes into your life that disturbs you, stop before you do anything unwise and take a minute out for consultation with your Maker to get His guidance. If someone offends you, before you say anything in anger, or even think inharmonious thoughts, stop to take just a minute for divine guidance instead of saying something you will be sorry for later. Let God's Spirit guide you to victory over inharmony by using Jesus Christ's method of returning good for evil.

No insult can overcome your peace of mind when you abide in God's love. With the light of divine guidance shining upon your affairs, you will find friends where before, in the shadows, you thought you saw enemies.

Paul gave the Corinthians some good advice concerning their attitude toward the divine source. This is what he wrote in his second epistle to them: "Wherefore we faint not; but though our outward man is decaying, yet our inward man is renewed day by day. For our light affliction, which is for the moment, worketh for us more and more exceedingly an eternal weight of glory; while we look not at the things which are seen, but at the things which are not seen: for the things which are seen are temporal; but the things which are not seen are eternal."

If we consider our right relationship to the visible world and to God and His invisible kingdom, as Paul has shown us, we shall understand how much more powerful is the power of God within us than the power of the external things that bother us in the world. By spending a minute with God, we can do more to free ourselves from the problems and the troubles of the world than we can do in days by fighting them with our human powers. If we seek the Truth, the Truth will make us free indeed.

Truth abides in the invisible Mind of God, which is eternal. Therefore, when we seem to be beaten and battered by the things of the outer world, let us take just a minute to abide in the eternal goodness and power of God.

There are two ways to deal with a problem: the personal way and the divine way. We usually take the most difficult way, which is the personal way. God's way is the easy way, but because of its simplicity we often feel that it is inadequate. When someone tells a lie about us, the personal way prompts us to contradict him and to make him retract the statement; the divine way shows us that there is nothing in a lie, that only the Truth is real. A realization of this fact without animosity toward the one who made the misrepresentation will erase the error from our minds, and will destroy the evil that might have become a reality to us if we had contended against it in a personal way. By thinking of the erring one as a child of God, we shall also help him to tell the Truth.

Remember that God's methods are love, meekness, forgiveness, harmony, peace, kindness, courage, fearlessness, energy, and truthfulness. No power of evil can stand against God's methods.

Seek God in the Silence

We must become receptive before we can receive God's answer to our prayers. God speaks to us in the silence. The silence means more than that we cease to speak with our lips; it means also that we must practice and maintain quietness in our mind and relaxation in our body. Sometimes when we are praying, we may not speak at all with our lips, but our mind is boiling over with emotions and negative fears so that we cannot hear the "still small voice" of God within us.

Our demanding will and our earthly ambitions must become quiet before we can receive God's instructions. When Jesus was asleep in the boat and a great storm on the sea disturbed His disciples, He rose up and stilled the wild waves by saying to them: "Peace, be still." When a storm of human emotions bursts upon us like a storm at sea, we must call upon the Christ within us to speak words of Truth that will bring peace and quietness into our consciousness.

Every one of us is a living temple of God. Paul wrote to the Corinthians: "Know ye not that ye are a temple of God, and *that* the Spirit of God dwelleth in you?" We must keep our temple peaceful and in order so that we may hear the still small voice of God. Elijah in the wilderness was able to hear the still small voice of God after the fire, wind, and earthquake had ceased. God was not in these noisy demonstrations of physical confusion, but when all became quiet, He spoke to Elijah in the still small voice. In Habakkuk we read: "But Jehovah is in his holy temple: let all the earth keep silence before him." This means that we should not let the cries of our earthly needs disturb the inner peace of our temple.

God is always with us, but we must also be with Him in Spirit before we can feel His presence. We can feel His presence if we will "be still, and know that I am God."

When Moses was leading the Children of Israel out of bondage from Egypt, the chariots of Pharaoh were behind them pursuing them and the Red Sea was before them. This situation caused the people to be very much confused and afraid. "And Moses said unto the people, Fear ye not, stand still, and see the salvation of Jehovah." They were then shown a way to pass through the Red Sea and were saved from the chariots of Pharaoh.

When we, like the Children of Israel, are faced with a dilemma in which we seem to be trapped between two difficulties, we should remember what Moses said to his people and say to our troubled thoughts: "Stand still, and see the salvation of Jehovah." There is always a way in which God can save us from our distress if we will stand still and let Him guide us.

When Jehoshaphat's people were facing the mighty hordes of the enemy, he was able to save them with the help of God. As it is written in 2 Chronicles, he said to them: "Fear not ye, neither be dismayed by reason of this great multitude; for the battle is not yours, but God's. . . . Ye shall not need to fight in this *battle:* set yourselves, stand ye still, and see the salvation of Jehovah with you." They followed these instructions and they were saved.

We can save ourselves from much unhappiness, worry, and even from doing the wrong things by standing still and seeing the salvation of Jehovah. When we do this, we shall be shown the right way to proceed.

Sometimes we go to God in prayer and then spend so much of our prayer time in telling Him about our troubles and in keeping our attention on them that we fail to give Him an opportunity to speak to us. God knows what we need before we ask Him, and it is more important for us to realize His presence and power than it is to tell Him about our problems. When we cast our burdens on God, we are set free from them. When we cast off our burdens and forget them, we shall be better able to hear His voice and to accept His answer to our prayer.

When we are full of negative thoughts, we have no room in us to receive God's blessings. When we ask God sincerely for His help, we must be willing to listen to His instructions. He will tell us that we do not have to fight for our good, but we must stand still and see the salvation of His Truth. We shall then know what to do.

We must first sacrifice our selfish feelings, our hates, fears, our jealous feelings, and our worries to God. Of course He is not interested in these worthless things. He loves us, but His love for us can be active in us only as we join Him in loving. As we work with Him in Spirit and in Truth we are able to enjoy His spiritual riches.

We must worship God in Spirit and in Truth. We cannot reach Him by trying to climb up to Him, using our troubles as a ladder. The first commandment tells us that we are to have no other gods before the one God. We may not think of our troubles as being our gods, but they are like idols, for to them we sacrifice our joy and peace of mind. Therefore, we worship false gods when we give our mind and heart over to fear and worry about the things of the world. The same thought power that we waste in worshiping the false gods of fear and worry could be used in worshiping God's love and good will.

Christ in us, if we will awaken Him, can still the storms of our troubled sea of thoughts and make it possible for us to hear the voice of God as He directs us into paths of peace, happiness, prosperity, and joy.

Patience Is a Winner

Quiet patience can and does master and outlive all boisterous, stormy human discords.

Patience is one of the expressions of God's love. Patience stills our human, selfish urge to follow the dictates of our personal will so that we can stop and listen to the beautiful spiritual guidance of our indwelling Christ. Patience helps us to enlarge our understanding of our surroundings so that we can find good in them. Patience shields us from suffering, from sudden reactions that make us angry, and restrains us from speaking discordant words. Patience helps us to succeed by refusing to acknowledge failure. This it does by causing us to wait on the Lord and to listen for His guidance before we do or say something that will interfere with the manifestation of our good before we have discovered that there is good in the thing that upsets us.

There is usually a better way to solve our worldly problems than our human intellect, unaided by divine guidance, can point out to us. We can find this better way when we stop worrying and patiently wait for divine understanding to show us the right way. When something disturbs us, if we will wait patiently before we say or do something foolish, we shall find peace of mind as well as wisdom. Patience will help us to find a way to meet discord without our entering into a state of mental discord.

Patience opens the way for us to perceive a larger view of life and its relationship to our world. Patience helps us to see beyond our personal limiting doubts, fears, and willful thoughts, and to behold the realm of Truth, love, and harmonious thinking. Our patience is founded upon our faith in God, a faith that makes us master of every situation.

God is always patient with us, His children. He forgives us for the mistakes that we make, but we cannot partake of the fullness and joy of His patient love while we fill our minds with impatient and willful thoughts. God does not punish His children. We punish ourselves by refusing to accept and to express His bounty of love and goodness. The prodigal son punished himself when he left his father and went into a far country, thinking that in this way he could get more pleasure out of his inheritance than he could by staying at home. Later he came to want because he had wasted his inheritance in riotous living, and he decided to go back to his father's house. His father ran to meet him with a kiss and welcomed him. His father was not angry, nor had he been angry with his son.

Our impatient ego self often drives us into a far country of worldly pleasures where we spend our God-given substance unwisely by leaving God out of our life. In such a case our unhappy experience reminds us to go back to our Father, who has always loved us and is patiently waiting for us to return and to enjoy His bounty.

By exercising our God-given power of patience, we can overcome the effect of any angry, condemnatory thoughts and words that other persons may send our way, and, instead, use our thought power to build up joy, health, happiness, and prosperity in our life and affairs. Patience endures while anger blows itself to destruction. Patience is the first requisite in the development of our spiritual understanding.

"Great peace have they that love thy law;
And they have no occasion of stumbling."

Patience gives us a larger view of the possibilities for good that are all about us. Where the impatient man sees failure and discouragement, the patient man sees new opportunities. Patience is a gift from God, which we receive by faith, and it helps us in every department of our daily living. Patience helps us to maintain self-control over our behavior so that we will always do the right thing. "Let us run with patience the race that is before us, looking unto Jesus the author and perfecter of *our* faith." One of the ancient writers, Plautus, who lived two hundred years before Jesus Christ, wrote: "Patience is the best remedy for every trouble." And in The Epistle of James we find: "And let patience have *its* perfect work, that ye may be perfect and entire, lacking in nothing." Henry Wadsworth Longfellow wrote:

> "God never changeth;
> Patient endurance
> Attaineth all things;
> Who God possesseth
> In nothing is wanting;
> Alone God sufficeth."

Another writer, François Rabelais, writes: "He that has patience may compass anything." William Shakespeare said: "How poor are they that have not patience!" In Psalms 37:7 (ASV) we find:

> "Rest in Jehovah, and wait patiently
>   for him:
> Fret not thyself because of him who
>   prospereth in his way,
> Because of the man who bringeth
>   wicked devices to pass."

Let us control ourselves by patiently waiting on the Lord. When something disturbs us, or when we are discouraged or unhappy, let us become quiet and be patient as we open our mind and heart to the divine current of God's love and guidance.

Will You Help to Restore Peace?

Peace and harmony were a part of God's original creation, for He did not create war or inharmony. These conditions exist only in the world of man. They cannot exist in God's perfect spiritual creation.

War on earth is the result of man's wrong thinking. Wrong thinking is the result of man's failure to realize his unity with God. Because he has not lived close to God's love and wisdom, he has lapsed into fear, greed, hatred, and misunderstanding. As a man finds his unity with his Father, God, his inharmonious states of mind vanish. As he cultivates faith in God's goodness and love, he automatically corrects his habits of wrong thinking and acting.

Since war is caused only by the thoughts in the minds of men, war can be eliminated only by a change in men's thoughts. This means bringing the thoughts of each individual back to God's way of thinking. Passing laws, building up armies, exploding atom bombs—nothing in the outer world can correct man's erroneous way of thinking, or stop war.

God's goodness and love and power are the only realities. These must be fully realized and incorporated into the minds of all men. Men must have the mind in them that was in Christ Jesus.

If men will erase wrong thinking from their minds and turn their attention toward God's real universe, the universe of Spirit, they can redeem the race from its bondage to the adverse appearances of the world, and they will then be free to enjoy the beauty of the realities of creation.

We are confused by many things about us that seem distorted to us because of our lack of clear spiritual vision. But when we clarify it and remember that God made all things good and that He is always with us, we begin to see a better world about us. It becomes beautiful and harmonious and the people in it more loving and cooperative. As we clarify our vision, we find that the kingdom of heaven is indeed at hand. The whole world may seem to others to be in an uproar, but when we realize our oneness with God, it is not so to us. When we unify ourselves with God and let Him direct our way, we walk in paths of peace and righteousness, we live in the good world that He has created. The storms of adversity that roar in the average man's world cannot disturb us, because we live in God's world, and these storms are not a part of it.

After thousands of years man is slowly growing up spiritually and is gradually learning to understand that he is not merely flesh but spirit also, a son of God and joint heir with Jesus Christ. When he is able to realize and understand the full meaning of this mighty Truth, he will not depart from his Father's house again, to dwell in a land of woe and strife.

When a man finds God within him by first finding his own Christ nature he no longer needs to fight evil. Man has been learning the hard way, by experience. So far he does not seem to have profited much by His hard experiences. Now is a good time for him to turn over a new leaf and stop searching in the wrong places for the answer to his needs. Let him now turn directly to the source of his life and existence and find the answer to all his questions in God, who will meet him more than halfway.

One man searching for God will find Him, but when a number of men join together in searching for Him, they exert a tremendous power for good in behalf of the whole race. Jesus said, "Where two or three are gathered together in my name, there am I in the midst of them." A few persons with faith in God can generate power enough to help many others to come into and enjoy God's kingdom.

However, to inspire the more than two billion people who live in the world with the power of God's loving helpfulness will require many times two or three working together in the name of Christ. There must be a definite and consecrated effort by a large number of enthusiastic, spiritually enlightened men and women if the world is to be freed from its ignorant, inharmonious thoughts and its people directed into a loving, powerful faith in the true, good world inhabited by good people that God created.

Men come to resemble what they believe in. Every man must learn to believe in his loving Father and to unify himself with the Father by loving Him with all his heart, soul, mind, and strength.

The question is raised in the 32d chapter of Deuteronomy as to how it is possible for one righteous man to "chase" a thousand and two righteous men to put ten thousand to flight. The answer is that it is possible because God can help the righteous men. With God's help, two righteous men can overcome ten thousand, and two affirmations of Truth can put ten thousand untrue statements to flight. God and Truth are the greatest powers in the universe.

Surely if two righteous men can overcome ten thousand, two hundred can overcome one million, and two hundred thousand can overcome one billion. This is nearly half of the total population of the world. No doubt a sufficient number of consecrated persons could be found among our readers to overcome the world of negative thoughts. Just think, a half million Truth students joining together in a realization of God's Truth in an endeavor to help the whole world overcome its wrong ideas about man and God and thus do away with strife, poverty, and sickness! This is a goal worthwhile.

Every man's wrong thoughts are his worst enemy, and Christ within him is his best friend, because Christ is the true Son of God, who can save every man, woman, and child from his wrong thinking. This Christ has been crucified by sin and neglect and is buried in material thoughts in nearly every man in the world. He must be resurrected in every person so that all people will know of a certainty that they are all brothers and sisters made in the image and likeness of their good and loving Father, God. When all men understand and believe in the Fatherhood of God they will feel and live in peace, prosperity, and happiness. Jesus reminded us that we are gods and sons of the Most High.

There are many more than the required number of sincere souls, I feel sure. If these will join in working to lift the world out of bondage to error into the freedom of Truth, I believe we can do it. This thing is possible because God is all-powerful, and when so many work with Him there can be no failure. Because righteousness is the only real and lasting condition in the universe, anything less is unreal, temporary, and unworthy of man's attention. This is why two righteous men have so much more power than ten thousand men who do not believe in their own divinity.

Will you, dear reader, be one of a host who will join in working to overcome the negative thinking in the world? The following statement has been suggested for us all to meditate upon in concerted spiritual unity of thought each day of this week:

The world which God created in the beginning was a good, harmonious world, and it is still a good, harmonious world, and it will always be a good, harmonious world.

The Spirit of Truth is now revealing this perfect world to me, and God is helping me to reveal its true character to many people. I agree with God's ideal, good creation and I am working with Him with all my heart, soul, and strength to bring His world into manifestation here and now.

Please read this statement over carefully until you enter into the universality of its spirit. Can you agree with its spirit, and do you believe the goal is attainable? Does it help you to realize how we can help God bring His kingdom onto the earth at this time? Those who undertake this work should cultivate perfect faith in the reality of God's spiritual creation as the only true creation.

With our attention fixed upon God as all-pervading love, harmony, power, wisdom, and peace, let us lay all thoughts about earthly problems aside and rest in His presence as we meditate upon this statement. Let us do this several times a day faithfully, spending as much time at each period as we can before our thoughts begin to wander. As you and a host of others who are joining with us begin to realize this great Truth, all of us will be brought closer to God and there is bound to be a definite uplifting and freeing effect produced in the consciousness of all the people in the world. God needs the help of all His children in working out His plans for their good in the manifest world.

Our goal seems to me to be most worthwhile, because it gets at the basic cause of man's difficulties, his attitude toward God and other men. In cooperating in this effort we are not only cooperating with one another but with Jesus Christ in bringing the kingdom of God into manifestation. It is not our desire to interfere with the freedom of anybody's thinking but only to help all men to become free from their age-old bondage of ignorant thinking about their relationship to God the Father. The promise is: "Ye shall know the truth, and the truth shall make you free." Jesus said: "Ye therefore shall be perfect, as your heavenly Father is perfect."

**I am still in the silence of my mind
and I am at peace.**

A Prayer Drill

First Day. *In Spirit and in Truth I am open and receptive to God's answer to my prayer.*

Second Day. *I stand still in the silence, that I may understand God's still small voice as He says to me: "Be still, and know that I am God."*

Third Day. *Christ in me calms the stormy waves of my human emotions as He commands: "Peace, be still."*

Fourth Day. *I listen for the voice of God, who is now in His holy temple, as I still all disturbing thoughts so that I can keep silence before Him.*

Fifth Day. *No worldly problems can disturb me, for I have faith enough to stand still and see the salvation of the Lord.*

Sixth Day. *The light of God surrounds me so completely that I see clearly His salvation.*

Seventh Day. *With silent assurance that God is all-powerful, I rest securely in His loving care.*

Chapter 11

Our Thought Messengers

**The Spirit of the Lord goes before me,
making safe, happy, and successful my way.**

You Are a King

YOU are the one who must decide what kind
of thoughts shall enter your mind. No one
else can enter into your mind and arrange
your thoughts for you.

It is true that others may be able to help you to
decide, but before they can do so, you must first
accept their constructive ideas and change your
thinking accordingly. If you refuse to accept their
ideas, they cannot help you.

God has given each individual the great responsibility of choosing his own thoughts and beliefs.
God is saying to each of us: "Choose you this day
whom ye will serve." We must decide for ourselves
what we shall believe in. The testimony of our
senses and the advice of other people may help us in
making our choice, but in the end we must make it
ourselves. We must each decide whether we will

believe the things of the world as they appear to be according to the testimony of our physical senses or whether we will believe the Truth, the Reality, as it is revealed to us by the Spirit of Truth that our Father has given us.

We must decide for ourselves whether by our attitude of hate and our fear thoughts we shall take up arms against what seems to be "a sea of troubles," or whether we shall call upon the Spirit of God to show us a better way to face these troubles. God will help us as He helped Moses and the Children of Israel when they faced a crisis, the sea before them and the Egyptians behind them. Moses changed his attitude toward these appearances from one of fear to faith in God, and said to his followers: "Stand still, and see the salvation of Jehovah." A dry path was provided through the sea for their safe passage to safety.

Every individual is a king in the castle of his own mind. As king of his thoughts he can think those thoughts which will make him an unhappy and fearful monarch, or he can make his reign joyous and harmonious by listening to the Father within himself before making decisions.

Jesus made this choice by deciding to let the will of the Father be done in Him rather than His own will. Thus He brought His rulership of His thoughts to the exalted standard of a perfect child of God. He would not allow appearances to influence Him to think thoughts of hatred, unforgiveness, or defeat.

Everyone must make his own decision as to whether he will accept the guidance of the Father or let outer events lead him into thinking disturbing, antagonistic, unhappy thoughts. When we let the Christ within us help us to rule our thoughts, we shall find that we have chosen the wise way, for then we shall rise above the confusion of the world of appearances with its fears and overcome its negative power to influence our righteous way of thinking.

In our daily life we are often disturbed by harmless noises. We allow noises of the physical world to enter into the kingdom of our mind to disturb our orderly thinking processes. We do this when we forget to exercise our spiritual dominion, our power to think powerful, constructive thoughts.

Some of us are made unhappy when we allow our attention to be diverted by noises in the neighborhood. Perhaps the noise may be a machine grinding, a jukebox blaring, an auto horn tooting, a child practicing on the piano, a dog barking, water dripping, the rattling of a window, the rapid tripping of an air hammer, a motor running, or even a chair squeaking. When we direct our attention to such things and agree that they do annoy us, our consciousness is so bound by this noise that we cannot think pleasant or constructive thoughts.

I had an experience recently that helps to illustrate how our attitude toward an offensive noise can be turned to a pleasant state of mind. On an airplane trip, while flying high above the clouds, I began to be conscious of the noise of the plane's motors. It had just occurred to me that they were making an unpleasant sound. I could not seem to think about anything but that noise and I did not like it. These unpleasant thoughts seemed to shut out all other thoughts from my mind. Then I realized that I was not taking the right attitude, so I relaxed, settled back, and began to think of the presence and harmony of God.

Suddenly the unpleasant roar of the motors seemed to change into the rich tones of a great pipe organ playing that grand old hymn, "Holy, Holy, Holy! Lord God Almighty," and then I heard the voices of a mighty choir joining in. The music was beautiful and restful and I listened to this and other uplifting hymns for more than an hour. I realized that the difference between the unpleasant sounds and the organ music was caused by my own changed attitude toward the sounds of the motors. When I forgot about the unpleasant noise and realized that God's harmony was present, I was able to hear God's harmony instead of earthly noise.

How often we may allow the disturbing conditions around us, which may consist of things other than noises, or offensive things that people are saying and doing, "get under our skin." Sometimes such conditions seem to grow more annoying from day to day but when we stop thinking about them and place them in God's hands, we change our attitude toward them so that we think of them as expressing God's goodwill. By so doing we can accept His harmony into our thinking. We can find that there is after all a divine order in these troublesome things, and that when we take the right attitude toward them they will bring good to us. We shall find harmony where apparently there had been only discord.

By right thinking we shall find that the kingdom of God is right here in our daily affairs. So let us be wise rulers of our thoughts and accept only those thoughts which are true in Spirit and in Truth.

What of Today?

At its beginning, today is like a clean sheet of paper before anything has been written upon it. This day's page is to be filled with your thoughts. What will they be like? Will they be the kind of thoughts that makes a nice-appearing page? You can fashion a beautiful day or an ugly day according to the kind of thoughts you think.

Your thoughts doubtless mostly concern things that are taking place outside of you, yet you have the privilege of thinking what you please about these things. We all walk under the same sun, but we do not all think the same thoughts about the sun. To some people the sun today is hot and oppressive, while others welcome it with praise and joy. Which of these two groups do you think gets the most out of today?

Every experience that comes into your life is greatly colored by your thoughts about it. But one thing is certain: Good, cheerful, pleasant thoughts in your mind make your day worth while. A disappointing experience is increased for you if you let your thoughts dwell upon the pain of it.

Some persons may think that they cannot control their thoughts. When they feel blue, they give up and just go on being blue. They think that is all there is to it and they cannot help it. But they can do something about it if they will try to control their thoughts. We are given the power to think in order to better ourselves and rise above difficulties.

If you would change conditions in your life, you must begin by changing your thoughts. If you would change your character, you must begin to change your daily thoughts, for your character is built around your thoughts. If you would be sweet and lovable so that others will seek your company, you must begin to think friendly, sweet, lovable thoughts.

To get yourself out of an unpleasant rut it is very

helpful to use some affirmation diligently and thus train your thinking processes to acquire the habit of good thoughts. Many Unity persons have learned "The Prayer of Faith" and find it very helpful to repeat the prayer often in order to lift their thoughts out of the old ruts and start them to building peace, power, and plenty in their life.

Here is "The Prayer of Faith," by Hannah More Kohaus. If you do not know it, use it and you will find help in it, and I suggest that you memorize it now. When depressing, ugly, weak, or fearful thoughts would mar your day, repeat this little prayer over and over and you will start a new train of good thoughts going across your page:

> God is my help in every need;
> God does my every hunger feed;
> God walks beside me, guides my way
> Through every moment of the day.
>
> I now am wise, I now am true,
> Patient, kind, and loving too.
> All things I am, can do, and be
> Through Christ, the Truth that is in me.
>
> God is my health, I can't be sick;
> God is my strength, unfailing, quick;
> God is my all; I know no fear,
> Since God and love and Truth are here.

Many persons have formed the habit of thinking negative affirmations such as: "I can't," "I am weak," "I don't know." These soil their pages and make bad days for these careless thinkers. They should replace these weak words with constructive prayers and strong, positive affirmations.

"The kingdom of God is within you," said Jesus, and it is possible for you to bring that kingdom into your life today through right thinking. A good affirmation to use when things seem to be going wrong is this:

"I open my mind to the loving presence of God, and all my affairs are in divine order."

These words will help you lift your thoughts above doubt, worry, and fear. Beautiful thoughts make a cheerful, happy today, a memory page that will be pleasant to look upon tomorrow.

If remembrances of old mistakes and regrets come to your mind, do not rehash them. Just drop them and begin thinking of something worth while instead. Do not let your today be marred by them. An old condition of the past cannot be helped now by your remorse, regret, or anger. Let it go and do not repeat it. Live each day with fresh joy and enthusiasm and fill it full of good thoughts.

Remember that God is with you now, at this moment, and that His goodness endures forever. Unify yourself with His goodness and see how beautiful you can make today. Shakespeare said:

"There's nothing either good or bad, but thinking makes it so." Improve each day by right thinking and the years will bring you good things.

God is with you when you are with Him, and you are with Him when you think good thoughts.

Thought Control

All things are created and now exist as ideas in the Mind of God. Creation includes the things that are invisible as well as the things that we can see.

The Bible tells us that God created all things by His Word. We know that ideas in the mind are the power and intelligence back of spoken words, so we therefore conclude that God's ideas must have created the universe. People who live in various parts of the world speak different languages and because of this, use words that are different to express the same idea. The idea is therefore more important than the words used to express it. We may be sure that "the Word" used by God to create the world describes the action of ideas in the Mind of God.

God's living, universal ideas are always with us. As we learn how to express these ideas in our thoughts and words, we are able better to understand how God's ideas can create in our mind the order and goodness that are in His mind. When we speak the words *God* and *Christ* with faith and humility, we bring into our minds the spiritual power that these names represent.

By faithfully repeating words of Truth, we can train and direct our thoughts so that they will be in accord with God's perfect ideas.

Our thoughts and words are the connecting link between us and God. God's Word, or His thoughts in action, is creative and perfect. Our words, or our thoughts in action, have creative power in our individual world. As we grow in spiritual understanding, we become more obedient children of God and learn to control our thoughts by thinking God's thoughts after Him.

The man who would control his own thoughts must first realize that God's ideas and thoughts are orderly and perfect, and then bring his own thoughts up to God's standard of perfection, which we call righteousness, by thinking in accord with the divine plan. The divine ideas of God constitute the divine plan, which is the will of God, the Father. Jesus Christ has told us: "The words that I say unto you I speak not from myself: but the Father abiding in me doeth his works."

The Father's perfect idea of man is the Christ. Jesus, the manifest man, unified Himself with Christ, the perfect Man. He has shown us how, by bringing this Christ-man idea into our own mind and letting it have dominion over our thoughts, we can control our thinking and will no longer need to fight evil thoughts. Paul tells us to "have this mind in you, which was also in Christ Jesus."

While our thoughts are creative, we have been given the freedom to use them as we please. Because they are creative and are continually changing our little world, we must learn to control our thoughts. We can make our world harmonious and good like the kingdom of God, or we can make it a world of discord and unhappiness. Isaiah said: "So shall my word be that goeth forth out of my mouth: it shall not return unto me void, but it shall accomplish that which I please, and it shall prosper in the thing whereto I sent it."

Even our idle words are creative. Jesus said in Matthew 12:36 (ASV): "And I say unto you, that every idle word that men shall speak, they shall give account thereof in the day of judgment." The day of judgment is today and every day. Each of us has proved this by experience. Again Jesus said: "For by thy words thou shalt be justified, and by thy words thou shalt be condemned."

Our need is to let the Christ Word dwell in us as stated in Colossians 3:16 (ASV): "Let the word of Christ dwell in you richly; in all wisdom teaching and admonishing one another with psalms *and* hymns *and* spiritual songs, singing with grace in your hearts unto God."

Since man has been given dominion that makes his every word creative, he has power to make manifest whatever he decrees. His spiritual nature and his spiritual thoughts and words have greater power than his negative thoughts and words. Jesus Christ said: "The words that I have spoken unto you are spirit, and are life."

We can best control our thoughts by letting the Christ words of *Spirit* and *life* come into our mind and expressing them through our spoken words. When we do this, we have not only put our thoughts in order but we have put our little world in order also.

If we think we must control our thoughts by means of our human will, we shall not be able to achieve true control over our thoughts. Our human will would advise us to fight against and condemn persons who speak negative words. Such condemnation and contention is a mistake that most of us make. Many persons interested in reform movements also make the same mistake. We spend too much of our thought energy in negative thoughts of condemnation and contention. We should not give our attention to the evil that we do not want and thus forget to think about the good that we do want. When we condemn wrong and are hateful and angry about the misdeeds of others, we must remember that the negative and destructive thoughts are in our own mind and that by expressing them we are building inharmony into our own little world.

We can overcome negative thoughts only by filling our mind with positive thoughts.

True reform comes to us when we let the Christ Mind come into and rule our mind. If someone does what we believe is evil and we try to destroy the evil by condemning him and making a disturbance about the evil he has done, we put our thought power into the business of creating more discord.

We cannot control our own thinking by making someone else change his way of thinking. We can accomplish more good by thinking thoughts of forgiveness and by trying to see the Christ in those who do wrong. Of course, we should not encourage anyone in wrongdoing. However, punishment alone cannot change the wrongdoer into a doer of good. The punishment may prevent him from doing something in the outer way, which solves only a part of the problem. When our mind is in order and controlled by God-Mind, our outer actions will be in order.

Most important of all, we must overcome hate with love. We must overcome evil with good. Of course, we have to "render . . . unto Caesar the things that are Caesar's and unto God the things that are God's," but if we stir up great discord in rendering unto Caesar the things that are his, we shall use up so much of our thought energy in doing so that we shall have no creative power left in us to render unto God what is His. If we render something unto Caesar, let it be done with forgiving love. By so doing, we can help God to put our mind in order.

A bad habit has its foundation in a bad habit of thought. A bad habit of thought overcome by sheer willpower will return with increased power unless a constructive habit is put in its place, or the vacant place may be taken by a worse habit. In overcoming faultfinding it is better to practice praise than to seal your lips. To overcome drinking intoxicating beverages, drink in the thought that Christ satisfies your every longing. All bad habits are but good impulses turned wrong. In the case of the faultfinder, the impulse is to have other people express perfection, but the method pursued is wrong. Perfection comes from praise and the finding of good, and not from the finding of faults.

The Little Foxes

Negative thoughts are like the little foxes mentioned in the Bible that destroy the vineyard. If such thoughts are not denied expression, they may grow in numbers and destroy a portion of the crop of good things that are growing into fruition in your life. God has planted fruitful vines in the vineyard of your soul; you must not let the little foxes of negative thought destroy them.

One little fox cannot do much harm, but if you encourage him by giving him your favorable attention, he may invite a horde of other foxes to come in and do a lot of damage to your crop of peace and happiness.

Spiritual good things are growing in your consciousness and should bring you much fruit. Some of these fruits of your vineyard are peace, joy, success, and satisfaction. You can protect and encourage this crop of good things by using good thoughts. Every thought you think adds something to the sum total of your consciousness. Your consciousness is built of the thoughts, ideas, and feelings that you have stored in it by your daily thoughts and reactions through the years. The good fruits of your inner vineyard grow into perfect spiritual maturity with the help of your mental creative process when it is in accord with Divine Mind.

Of course the nature of your consciousness is changing to some degree every day as you change the character of your thoughts and your mental attitude toward the things that come into your life experience. When you persist in following a certain trend of thought, your consciousness becomes definitely colored and influenced by that trend. The optimist has a pleasant outlook on life as compared with the pessimist, who has a dark outlook. The consciousness of each is colored light or dark according to his outlook. One has more sunshine and the other more shadow in his soul consciousness, each according to his own outlook.

But just being an optimist is not enough to produce an abundant crop of good fruit. You must also train yourself to look for and discover the good in everything that happens to you and find a way to make use of this good by blessing it in your thoughts, words, and actions. Do this with the faith that God's omnipresent wisdom and power are helping you.

Do not let the bad habit of negative thinking grow on you. It may start in a harmless kind of a way. You may begin by looking critically at a few negative points in your associates; you may not like something that someone is doing or the way he wears his hat or the tone of his voice. It is always possible to find something in nearly everybody to criticize, but there is always more good in everybody than bad.

You can always find and enjoy something good in every person if you look for it. When you discover this good and make the most of it, even if you do not mention it, glory will be added to your inner vineyard. But when you pick at the faults in anyone who annoys you, a shadow flits across your consciousness.

Suppose a group of people go into a beautiful garden where there is much to please the eye and to praise, but one of the group, who has developed a habit of negative thinking, searches among the roses and discovers a worm on which he concentrates his attention and interest.

Its appearance shuts out the beauty of the garden for him as he shudders at the unpleasant experience of watching this ugly worm. The time that he spends in viewing this ugly sight might just as well have been used to enjoy the roses and the beautiful things in the garden. The beautiful Garden of Eden was filled with good things, but Adam and Eve chose to concentrate their attention upon the fruit of the tree of good and evil.

Hunting for worms by the gardener in order to cast them out is quite different than when a guest who has come to enjoy the beauty of the garden calls attention to them.

Cultivate the habit of looking for the good things of life and of praising these things as you enjoy them, and you will be happy.

It is just as easy to find and enjoy these things as it is to complain about the unlovely things; in fact, it is much easier, because there are so many more good things in life than bad.

If there is something wrong and you can fix it, it is right to give it attention while you fix it, but to indulge the bad habit of looking for flaws and dwelling upon them when you cannot remedy them actually hurts you more than it hurts anyone else. Thinking about mistakes, troubles, disappointments, slights, and grudges opens the gates of your consciousness to the little foxes that destroy the fruit of your God-given vineyard.

God is a good, loving Father and He is everywhere present. Look for Him everywhere you go and you will find His goodness in the most unexpected places. The power of His love working through you will shut the gate against the little foxes. They can have no power to destroy your vineyard unless you give it to them by your negative attitude toward life.

It seems easy to say, "So-and-so has snubbed me and I am miserable," and it is easy to criticize a person's manners or the cut of his hair, but such thoughts are not helpful. We must learn to rise above negative thinking and keep the little foxes from eating up our store of good thoughts.

One bad habit that opens the way for a pack of little foxes to come into your vineyard is to count your troubles instead of your blessings. Your problem cannot destroy your good, but your negative thinking about your problems *will* destroy your good.

Thinking about unpleasant things instead of praising the power of God's goodness destroys the good fruit of your vineyard. Many people today are carrying around in their heart heavy burdens that they do not need to carry. They take upon themselves unnecessary worry burdens that are heavier than their duties.

It is right to think about ways to solve your problems but your thoughts about these problems must be positive and be backed by the assurance that you can solve them by the help of God's power and wisdom. You must learn to cast your burdens on the Lord. When your negative thoughts are turned over to God, they become as nothing, and if it is necessary for you to do something, it will be shown you. You do not need to carry the heavy excess baggage of negative thought, for God will show you what to do if you will let Him, and He will also give you strength to do it.

The greatest burden that you have to bear is the burden of your own belief in the evils that you think you see. You can just as well work with constructive ideas that will protect your vineyard from the little, destructive thought foxes.

The best way to deal with these little foxes is to remember that God's good words are always with you, waiting for you to express them in thought, word, and action. Think with God, and let the little foxes go back into the wilderness of unreality from which they came.

How to Master Self-Consciousness

You have no cause to be confused at any time, and you will not be confused unless you allow your personal self to monopolize your thoughts. You should avoid dwelling upon thoughts about personal traits that cause your embarrassment. Think about the good you desire to manifest instead of about things you fear or dislike.

The members of the human family are on the whole so much alike in fundamental qualities that none of us needs to become disturbed because of his fancied inferiority in the presence of others.

If a person keeps his poise, he will not seem to be awkward or out of place anywhere. But if he loses his poise by thinking about his handicaps, he will become self-conscious, advertising this fact by his nervous behavior and thus drawing to himself the very adverse attention that he dreads.

A child of God has no need of being self-conscious. Remember that you are a child of God. If you will concentrate your attention upon the thing you are doing, forgetting your human personality, you will be natural and charming.

Humility is a charming grace that is appreciated by all. A person who is self-conscious often believes he is humble because he depreciates himself, but in fact he is seldom truly humble. He thinks so morbidly about his personality that he is unable to get an accurate perspective of his relationship to others. One moment he raises his personality to the heights and the next moment he lowers it to the depths. If he cannot personally be superior to others, he is so disappointed that he feels inferior to all.

Self-consciousness is a form of conceit. The truly humble man is one who looks out upon life with poised and peaceful mind. Comparison of his own appearance and standing with those of others does not upset his equilibrium. While he is humble, he does not think of himself as being inferior. He is open-minded and ready to accept improvement at all times, but he is not unhappy about his present status. He does not condemn himself because he seems to know less than someone else or because he is not the equal of a neighbor in good looks.

No one should be miserable because he feels inferior. There is One in you who is inferior to no human being: your Christ Self. If you are a person who worries about being inferior, you should begin at once to forgive yourself for thinking bad thoughts about a child of God. If you will always remember that in Spirit you are a child of God and that everyone else is also a child of God, you will begin to realize that you are a member of a large, loving family, and you will not feel ill at ease in the presence of anyone.

Each individual has his particular God-given gifts that he should cultivate and develop to their highest degree. Everyone must be himself, which means that he must be the best "self" of which he is capable. You should thank God continually for life, love, intelligence, beauty, and harmony, which are yours to use abundantly. As you give thanks for these things and praise them, they will begin to unfold and expand, and you will daily become a better expression of the particular good qualities that have been given you by the Father. The sunflower does not worry because it is not a rose; neither should a person with certain gifts worry because he does not have gifts just like those which others seem to have. What a drab world it would be if everyone expressed just the same qualities!

It takes all kinds of persons to round out a world. Every individual has a number of talents that he has not yet fully developed and that would bring him much pleasure if he would develop them. Instead of condemning yourself because you do not have another's outstanding characteristic, you should give thanks that you are a charming, efficient, radiant child of God expressing your talents in your own natural way. When you realize that Christ is the real Self of you, then you will know that you are superior to embarrassing situations. The personal self of you will react in a peaceful and harmonious way toward all experiences when you are directed by the Christ within you.

Never be discouraged because any other person

has achieved something that you have not; rather, work joyously to bring out the faculties that God has given you. Do not try to imitate other persons. Give thanks when someone develops a good gift, because he is proving that you can make your gifts splendid also. Be on friendly terms with all good, developed gifts. Do not be unfriendly toward any good work just because you did not do it. Resentment never brought anything good out of a soul, but blessing a good quality, even though it may belong to someone else, will help you to develop some good talent in your own life.

Your Younger Brother

Did he slip and fall,
Or was his progress hid behind a hill
    before he reached the top?
Condemn him not because he has not
    reached the heights.
(The green fruit needs but sun to
    make it ripe.
Do not mistake the green grape for
    the bad.)
Condemn him not, but help to guide
    his way by kindly word and noble
    deed.
He passes through the valley on his
    way toward the peak.

Call out to him with friendly word
    and guide him to the goal.
A rope thrown out will bring him to
    the top safely more than a stone
    rolled down upon his path.

God Has a Wonderful Plan for You

Remember that God is a loving Father and that, because He loves you, He has made a perfect plan for you.

His plan, if you follow it, will help you to succeed and to be happy, prosperous, harmonious, and healthy. His plan will help you to go safely through all the difficult experiences that may challenge you in the world. God does not force you to follow His good plan, but He is lovingly waiting for you to accept it and to let Him walk with you in the way.

Because He is your loving Father, He does not punish you if you refuse to follow His good plan. But if you do not follow it, your own plan, followed without God's help, may cause you to make many unwise decisions and mistakes.

Jesus' parable of the prodigal son can help us to understand how our Father-God loves us so much that He gives us freedom to leave the blessedness of our Father and go into a far country of our own choice to seek for our happiness in selfish ways. Our journey into a far country may follow a plan that we think will bring us happiness in the world without the help of God. When our plan fails and we come to want, we can always change our mind and return to our heavenly Father's house. He is always ready to receive us with a loving welcome and to let us enter into His good plan.

If today we are traveling in a far country where we are finding poverty and unhappiness, we can stop and come to ourselves and remember that we are a son of God, and thereupon return to our Father's house. The prodigal son decided to go back to his Father's house and become a servant. The wayward son returned with a meek spirit, ready to become a servant in his father's house, but his father received him with love as a son who had been lost.

In order to enter into God's plan for us, we must become meek. When we are meek toward God, we do not need to feel that we are not as good as other people, but our meekness should help us to give up our own selfish plans and desires so that there will be room in us to receive God's ideas. When our minds and hands are full of our own inharmonious ideas, we cannot open them to take hold of God's wonderful plan. In order to make room in our life for God's plan, we must relax and let go of our negative ideas. In this way we come with open minds and hearts to receive His goodness.

The Father's perfect way for us is a way of joy, happiness, prosperity, health, and harmony. As we follow God's plan, we walk in the right way. Today, as we drive down a road, we often see a sign that reads: "Keep right." This is also a good instruction to follow when we seek to follow God's plan in life. To go the right way we must be willing to give up our personal ideas. When we follow the selfish, human way, because we are afraid of others, we may become angry, dictatorial, or egotistical as we seek the applause of men. These attitudes of mind may lead us into rough paths, because we are not following God's good plan. God's plan is a very smooth way in which we enjoy the beauty of harmony, peace, and forgiveness.

To follow God's plan we must forgive our enemies and love them instead of fighting them. We should not become angry and run away from our good because we are afraid. We should remember that the love of God is stronger than all the negative conditions in the world.

God's plan lifts us above the rough places of the world as we joyously share our good with others. The first commandment is that we must love God with all that is within us. When we do this, we stir up God's gift of love in our consciousness so that it flows out to all our neighbors; and the more we share it, the more it expands.

The joy of the Lord is our strength and when we stir up the joy that God has put within us and express it, it will be reflected back to us from all outer things. Joy does not come to us from things, but it comes through us from God to shine on all things.

We have been given muscles in our body, but unless we use them, they will not develop. So it is with the blessings that God has given us. These blessings include joy, harmony, peace, and love. They are all included in the good plan that God has prepared for us. When we give thanks and rejoice as we move along in God's plan and well-being, no difficult situation that arises can turn our personal feelings away from God's plan. When something in our life seems to go wrong, we should relax and let God show us the loving, harmonious way to handle the situation.

God's plan leads us to do that which is good for all concerned as well as for ourselves. Therefore, let us rejoice continually as we work with God with all the power that is within us. When we let God's wisdom, love, power, and joy express themselves in us, we become new creatures in Christ Jesus.

**The Spirit of the Lord goes before me,
making safe, happy, and successful my way.**

A Prayer Drill

First Day. *I create good in my life and in my
affairs by thinking good thoughts about others.*

Second Day. *I cannot afford to think unhappy
thoughts about other persons and about my affairs,
because such thoughts are seed that bear fruit after
their kind. Therefore, I will plant only good seed by
thinking only good thoughts.*

Third Day. *As I forgive those who seem to be my
enemies, I fill my soul with joyous friendship.*

Fourth Day. *I agree with the Christ Spirit, which,
I know, abides in everybody.*

Fifth Day. *Let the words of my mouth and the
meditations of my mind be in accord with the Christ
standard.*

Sixth Day. *I am blessed by every kind thought that
I think about myself and other persons.*

Seventh Day. *The Christ Mind in me is my hope of
glory.*

Chapter 12

Health Is Yours

I am Spirit, and Spirit cannot be sick.

Healing the Body

CHRISTIAN healing means more than patching up a broken body. It means restoring a body to its God-planned perfection— the harmonious manifestation of God's perfect-man idea in a physical body.

God's perfect man is Spirit, because God created him in His own image and likeness, and God is Spirit. This perfect spiritual man is the Christ, whose Spirit dwells in potential expression in the physical body of every man.

God's spiritual ideas find expression in the manifest world. God's perfect-man idea became manifest as a physical man formed from the dust of the ground. He became a living soul when God breathed the spirit of life into his nostrils.

The breath of life in man is God's life-idea in action. God's perfect-man idea is the pattern that all men must eventually work out in their physical bodies as Jesus did. Man's body can be self-renewing, even without the aid of his conscious mind, because his body is obedient to the orderly plan that God breathes into it. It is up to each person to cooperate with God's plan by letting the perfect-man idea, the Christ Spirit within himself, have its perfect way.

Man's lack of cooperation with God's wise and loving plan will often cause interference in the smooth working of God's will in his body; but even when a person does not fully cooperate with God's plan, restoration continues in his body, healing cuts and bruises and repairing any other damage that may be inflicted on the body.

As we increase our faith in the Christ perfection in us, we cooperate with God to bring more and more of His perfect-man idea into manifestation in our body. John the Baptist said: "He that believeth on the Son hath eternal life." Christ gives us eternal life, which we accept by having faith in Him. We can increase our faith in Jesus Christ by transferring our faith from outer things to the reality of the Christ in us. Let us become a new creature in Christ Jesus through faith.

Jesus said that all things are possible to those who believe in Him and in the works that He did. These works include His demonstration that physical man is a manifestation of the Son of God. We must believe that Christ is the living reality in our life as Christ was the living reality in Jesus' life. Jesus had such perfect faith in the power of His Christ self that He was able to heal the sick and to raise the dead, and He said that those who believe on Him (the Christ within themselves) will be able to do even greater works than He did.

In order to follow Jesus in the regeneration and realize our healing, we must quicken our faith in the divine power of God's Son in us and prove our divine sonship as Jesus did.

Affirmations of Truth are statements that describe God's perfect creation. By believing that God's creation is perfect and is the only reality, we can manifest it in our life. By using affirmations of Truth, we increase our faith in God's goodness becoming manifest here and now in our life and affairs.

We can affirm the Truth of our relationship to God until we feel its reality. We must first accept the truth in our mind, and then we shall be able to cooperate with the divine wisdom and life that are already at work in us to bring peace, health, and happiness into our body and affairs. By faithful use of affirmations of Truth, we can lift our body into a consciousness of greater harmony with its spiritual Source. Try using this affirmation: *By the healing power of my indwelling Christ I am made whole and perfect in mind and body*. Have faith that these words are true, because you are speaking the truth about God's perfect man.

We must train ourselves to have faith in our

indwelling Christ, who is whole and perfect. We must
have faith in God's perfect, spiritual, everywhere-
present creation, even though we cannot see it with
our physical eyes. We must learn to look for good
everywhere and thus open the way for God's spiritual perfection to come into our world as it is in His
heaven.

God's desire is for us to manifest perfection in
our bodies so that we can become His happy,
healthy children. He has given us access to all His
spiritual blessings, but we must cooperate with Him
by being willing to accept and use His wonderful
gifts through faith and love.

Affirmative prayer is our first step in seeking
God and His kingdom. By using affirmations of
Truth we pray constructively, as His children
should; not negatively, as beggars. As we grow spiritually by increasing our love and faith in God and
His perfect creation, we shall be able to find His
blessings everywhere. We shall find that health,
happiness, and prosperity are always with us. God is
our health; and when we believe this, His healing
power will work freely through us.

Curing Colds

Health or bodily ease is a normal state of being.
Disease is unnatural. Man's body is intended by the
Creator to be healthy, harmonious, and perfect.

God created a perfect spiritual man in the beginning. Surely such a man should live in a perfect body. Imperfections in the body can occur only when the human mind is not fully cooperating with the perfect spiritual man. The mind of the individual influences the state of health in the body. Disorder in any part of the body indicates a wrong attitude in the mind.

The body is a unit, and disorder in any part lowers the efficiency and well-being of the whole body. Take, for instance, a cold in the throat: what a disturbance it is to one's general comfort.

The average person usually attributes the cause of a cold to outer circumstances. Seldom does he think of the cause as being in his inner thoughts. Certain dietitians now teach that the individual is responsible for his own colds because of improper eating habits. They say that overeating or wrong combinations of foods may cause poisons to be deposited in certain parts of the body, especially in the mucous membranes, and these poisons produce colds. We are told by others that when the leucocytes, the "police" corpuscles in the blood stream, attempt to throw the virus or poison out of the system, congestion results.

Nearly everyone agrees that a cold is a congestion, the blood rushing to an infected part, making it throb with fever and slough off matter that is called by various names. In a congested part, some

kind of battle seems to be taking place. The healthy
body cells are apparently fighting disease germs, or
poison, and in doing so great numbers of them are
destroyed and become phlegm. The whole trouble
seems to be caused by some sort of unnatural activity in the local part, perhaps the tonsils or the nose.
The question arises "What causes this inharmony?"
How can a draft of air blowing on a person's head
cause the cells in his nose to get into such a jam? A
draft could never do it unless the directive forces of
the mind and the body aided it.

The life forces of the body are normally nicely
balanced, but this balance can be upset by fear,
worry, anger, or various other negative emotions. A
subconscious fear of cold air will cause trouble. If
cold air be met with a feeling of love and pleasure
instead of fear, no harm will result. We should learn
to go forth and meet God's fresh air with joy
instead of shrinking from it.

If there is confusion or congestion in some part
of your body that is making you weak and unfit to
enjoy yourself, the logical course for you to pursue
is to bring about peace and harmony in that section. Since inharmony of this sort is caused by
wrong thinking, it can only be cured by right
thinking.

Go in thought to a congested locality in your
throat or head and repeat quietly: "Peace. The love
of God is at work here. My life forces are peaceful

and harmonious. There is no resistance in me against the Spirit of God's pure, peaceful life." Quietly and lovingly attract the attention of your disturbed cell members and impress upon them the Truth that they are a part of the expression of God's harmonious life. Think of the free-flowing life of God being equalized throughout your entire body, doing away with all congestion. Assure your obedient servants, your blood corpuscles and body cells, that everything is all right and that they can go back to their normal activities. Free them from bondage to the idea of friction and discord. Become peaceful and then you will be able to reach them with your words of Truth. You can produce public sentiment among your body cells in favor of peace and harmony that will relieve all congestion. But this can be done most successfully after you are at peace with your neighbors and the whole world.

Free yourself from the erroneous ideas back of a cold. Become free from anger, worry, and all disquieting emotions. In this way you will establish equilibrium throughout your whole body.

Practice continuous harmonious thinking, and when you are able to maintain a quiet, peaceful state of mind under all circumstances, you will not have to meet any more resistant conditions in your body.

Relax your mental and physical tension so that God can do His perfect work in you. God's life in you is always good. Accept the reality of this good life and let its free, healing power flow evenly through your whole system.

Affirm: *The love and peace of Jesus Christ fill my body. No congestion can interfere with the expression of His pure life.*

No draft of air can cause me discomfort. I love the air and the breeze, and they can bring me only good.

My life forces work harmoniously together and produce health in my body.

You and Your Body

Remember that your body is "a temple of the living God." Because this is true, you have the great responsibility of keeping it in order, clean, pure, beautiful, and holy, and in every way fit for God's occupancy.

It is interesting to note that when you keep your body fit for God, you are also keeping it fit for your own use and enjoyment. One who believes that enjoyment comes as a result of indulging his sense appetites very often makes his body unfit for God to dwell in, and in thus treating his body, he also makes it unfit for his own soul to live in.

Your body is a very necessary member of the trinity that makes up your being. You would not be a complete being without a body. You are Spirit, soul, and body, three parts, or expressions, of the divine-man idea, in one. These three must become unified in order that you may become a perfect expression of God's ideal man. By lifting up your body, seeing it as Spirit substance instead of matter, you help to unify it with your true spiritual nature. By lifting up your opinion of your body, you aid it to attain its divine inheritance. You will thus gain an understanding of the true peace, joy, and dominion that are yours as a son of God.

Your body is dependent upon Spirit for its life, intelligence, and substance, and the further it is separated from the Spirit by your materialistic ideas concerning it, the less will it manifest life, intelligence, and substance. The farther you sit from the reading lamp in your home, the less light you will have to read by. When you feel that your body is something apart from God, it enjoys but dimly the radiating light of Spirit.

Your body is more than flesh, blood, and bone. It is an expression of divine ideas of life, substance, and intelligence. If your body did not have intelligence, it could not repair cuts in its skin and knit together its broken bones. If it did not have intelligence, it would not know how to grow from a little child into a man or woman. If it did not have intelligence, it could not operate the wonderful laboratory that digests its food and turns it into flesh, blood, bone, hair, fingernails, energy, brains, and other useful things that you need. Without intelligence it could not keep your heart beating and your blood circulating, even while you sleep.

Your body receives vitalizing instructions from Spirit, but it accepts your personal suggestions also. When you tell it that it is tired, it believes you. You do not have to say, "Body, you are tired," in so many words, but the very thought that you have in the back of your mind, the idea that your body is material and subject to weariness, means that you are making that suggestion to it.

Nearly all of us do suggest to our body every day that it is growing older and that it is subject to decay and disease. Some people are suggesting to their hearts that they are weak. Some are suggesting to their brains that they cannot remember things. In the Apocryphal New Testament we read (in III Hermas 5:58, 59): "Keep this thy body clean and pure, that the Spirit which shall dwell in it may bear witness unto it, and be judged to have been with thee. Also take heed that it be not instilled into thy mind that this body perishes." This is good advice, and even though it is in the Apocrypha and not in one of the canonical books of the Bible, it was no doubt written by a person of insight, for it harmonizes with Truth.

If there is an organ or function in your body that seems to be below par, lift up your thoughts concerning it. By lifting up your thoughts, I mean dedicating this organ or function to the Christ perfection. This will tend to restore it to its original perfection.

Back of your body is the perfect, ideal body created in the image and likeness of God. By lifting up your thoughts about your body in praise and thanksgiving and realizing that it is indeed a spiritual body, you will help to bring it into its true estate. The Scriptures say:

> "There is a spirit in man,
>   And the breath of the Almighty
>   giveth them understanding."

Bless your body and dedicate it to God's service each day, realizing that the vitalizing life of the Spirit of God is pulsating through every atom and fiber of it, healing, cleansing, and making it perfect. Realize also that God is your life, strength, and substance, and that no material conditions can harm God's substance. When your body is lifted up in consciousness to its rightful place, it will be filled with light and healing. Cooperate with the forces of spiritual life and intelligence by setting your body free from your worry thoughts about it.

> "Ye are gods,
>   And all of you sons
>   of the Most High."

I am Spirit, and Spirit cannot be sick.

A Prayer Drill

First Day. *Because my body is a temple of the living God, I am keeping it holy to His name.*

Second Day. *I am thankful because God's life, substance, and intelligence are sustaining and glorifying my body.*

Third Day. *My heart is right with God.*

Fourth Day. *Every day I rededicate my body to God's service.*

Fifth Day. *God is my life, and because His life is abundant, my life is abundant.*

Sixth Day. *The substance of my body is not subject to sin and disease, because it is an expression of divine substance.*

Seventh Day. *I bless my body and lift it up in my esteem because it is a temple of the living God.*

Chapter 13

Getting Along With Others

The Christ in me greets the Christ in you.

Our New Neighbors

THE commandment "Thou shalt love thy
neighbor as thyself" was given by Jesus Christ
many years ago. We today must apply it to a
much larger number of neighbors than the people
who heard Jesus could have imagined.

In those days of limited methods of travel and
communication, a man's neighbors were confined
to those persons who lived within a radius of a few
miles. However, Jesus made it clear that a man's
neighbors were not limited to persons living in his
own country, for He explained to His listeners that
a man from the despised country of Samaria could
also be considered a good neighbor.

Today the bounds of our neighborhood are
spreading so rapidly that our neighbors will soon
include the inhabitants of the whole world. People
who live on the other side of the world are neighbors
of ours today, because of the fact that we are aware

of them and, in many cases, they are affecting our way of life through commerce, travel, printed matter, and war.

Though some of our neighbors may be separated from us by thousands of miles, they are daily coming closer to us through the media of radio, television, airplanes, and modern methods of land and sea travel. It is not unusual today for us to see and hear what people are doing on the other side of the world right while they are doing it.

What modern television is bringing us is marvelous. Television is a modern miracle produced by science, and yet it is not the ultimate means of our knowing our distant neighbors better. Through improved scientific devices of man, we shall continually be brought closer to the people who live at the ends of the earth, but these devices will help us eventually to understand the Truth, namely, that all people are already one in Spirit.

Spirit can give us a better understanding and way of cooperation than television or radio or any other material man-made device. Because it is controlled largely by consideration of things in the material world, our present consciousness keeps us from knowing how very close we are to all our neighbors. When we truly love God and our neighbors, we become unified with everybody in peaceful friendship. We are all one in the perfect, spiritual man that God created in His image and likeness in the beginning. When we attain this consciousness of unity, we shall better understand how closely we are related to all people.

God-Mind is omnipresent. Spiritual ideas therefore move in God-Mind faster than light. God's idea of love is omnipresent. It needs only our acceptance and use of it to bring us into contact with it in other persons, even though they may be in distant lands. It is necessary for us to realize our unity with God's love in our neighbor, for it is able to bring us all together in unity of purpose. When we abide in God's love, which is within ourselves, we are at that instant at one with God's love in all peoples. Thus we see how God's ideas move faster than radio waves.

In our present limited state of consciousness, we are prone to be suspicious and afraid of newly found neighbors, and we therefore set up barriers between them and ourselves. When divine order is established in our affairs through our acceptance and use of divine love, the barriers will disappear, and we shall be able to work more efficiently together with our neighbors, here or abroad.

There are things that others can do better than we can, and there are other things we can do better than they can. When we work in a loving and orderly way and are not afraid of others, we are able to cooperate with them by doing the service we love to do and can best do, and thus we become happy servants of others because we are servants of God.

The day is not far off when God's servants will do their work to His glory and the spiritual uplift of their fellowmen. No one will then be afraid that his good may be taken away from him, but everyone will work joyously and produce what he loves to produce, and will then exchange his surplus for the surplus of others who do other things.

Everyone has a talent and something to offer to others. We shall someday no longer be afraid that the products of our neighbors who live in foreign countries will deprive us of our good.

In the very process of becoming acquainted with our neighbors today, we are finding much that disturbs us. Because we do not understand our neighbors, we are afraid of them, and as a result we have wars and troubles. It seems a roundabout way to get acquainted with our neighbors when we do it through strife and trouble. Such a means of introduction is indeed crude, but it will lead eventually to world unity if and when people everywhere learn the Truth about themselves and God.

As we approach the goal of universal brotherhood, we are entering into new and more difficult problems. We are meeting our neighbors in most instances the hard way, by the way of war and strife. Our problem is to unify all people with us by first unifying ourselves with God. The present troubles of the world are the birth pangs of a new and unified world in which there will be no more fear, hate, or war, a world in which there are no enemies, for all will be good neighbors.

We who are learning to understand Truth should steadfastly maintain our poise as we practice more faithfully to maintain a consciousness of God's love, no matter what may happen. By so doing, we shall speed the coming of the day of universal peace.

We must avoid thoughts of fear, hate, criticism, and condemnation as we keep close to the saving power of God's love through the Christ within us. We must do more than repeat with our lips the Lord's Prayer; we must be coworkers with Jesus Christ in bringing order, peace, goodwill, and prosperity onto the earth by thinking, speaking, and doing everything as if we were living in the kingdom of heaven now.

Wisdom falls short without love. Love is a constructive force. Love is the secret power in growth. Love brings men together in cooperation. Love causes a man to think of the welfare of other men. This is one of the fundamentals of success. No man who thinks only of his own selfish interests can be truly successful.

Love does not destroy; it upbuilds. Love wins battles that force cannot hope to win, for it destroys its enemies by changing them into friends; force attempts to destroy its enemies by killing them.

Force fails in its purpose, because it would destroy; love wins, because it would construct. Force would destroy the man; love would keep the man, and change the condition. An enemy is one who does not understand you, and one whom you do not understand. Love draws your Spirit close to his Spirit, and shows you that his heart yearns for truth, honesty, justice, life, and love, just as your heart yearns for these things. Love shows you that you are brother to all men, and that it is more blessed to give than to receive. If you have an enemy, it is at least half your fault.

Love is not a negative, idle force that mourns when it is neglected; it is positive and it reaches out, including all in its embrace. It conquers all, but subjects none.

Getting Even

You cannot get even with a person who has offended you by offending him in retaliation. Because someone else misbehaves is no reason why you should misbehave.

If someone calls you an unsavory name, you can hardly get even with him by saying, "You're another!" But you can maintain your peace of mind, poise, and self-respect by giving him a sincere silent blessing.

There is often a feeling among children and sometimes among grownups, too, that you must give the offender back in kind what he gives to you. In this way you are supposed to get even with him. However, it does not seem logical to reason that you can better yourself by duplicating another person's wrong deed.

Every spiteful word or deed you speak or do places you on a lower level than the loving, friendly level of happy living. If you stoop to get even with a man who has done something you do not like, surely you are lowering yourself to his level. In this sense you will be getting even with him.

Why not be a lifter instead of a depresser? Jesus said: "And I, if I be lifted up from the earth, will draw all men unto myself." Everyone who lifts up the Christ consciousness in himself will draw others up to a higher level of consciousness.

A person who understands how to apply the power of the Christ Word can counteract the human tendency to practice retaliation. He can do this by raising his own level of spiritual consciousness.

Paul's advice was that we should not try to overcome evil with evil, but that we should overcome evil with good. When we stand firmly on the solid foundation of faith in God's goodness, we are able to lift others up so that they can see the light of His goodness and by this light avoid sinking into lower

levels of consciousness. But if we follow in the foot-
steps of those who walk in darkness, we shall sink
with them.

There is great need in the world today for all men
to maintain a high standard of conduct, not in the
world of appearances alone, but in the world of spiritual reality, which is the true character of man. The
Christ Spirit abides in everyone, whether he realizes
it or not. Therefore, we must look within to this
Christ goodness for guidance instead of following
the example of those in the world who are practicing the old, traditional ways of the caveman.

Jesus Christ is the Saviour of the world, and to be
saved we must follow Him and not those who are
going down in the darkness. We must turn our
attention to the light of Christ, which leads us up
to the heights where we are saved from the dark
places below. When we are in this high state of consciousness, those who are in darkness will not be able
to offend us. We shall not be insulted or made unhappy about anything that happens in the consciousness of a person whose level of consciousness is lower
than our own. Let us therefore be wise and consider
how much better it is to lift up our would-be tor-
mentors than to fall into their misguided ways.

The world today needs men and women who are
able to stand steadfast in Truth and help those who
are stumbling, men and women who can forgive
and enlighten those who are making mistakes

instead of condemning them or following their bad example, men and women who will let their light shine by thinking better thoughts and doing better deeds. This world in which we live affords us amazing opportunities, because here it is possible for us to find the kingdom of heaven or its opposite, right where we are.

Man finds heaven by lifting up the Christ in himself, allowing the Christ light to shine into all his affairs. Whether he realizes it or not, everyone who lifts his own vision toward the Christ consciousness is helping to lift the vision of others. He also is helping to lift the world consciousness out of its nightmare of fear, hatred, greed, and those other states of mind which cause war and unhappiness. So let us who know the Truth be alert to set a good example for those who are making the mistake of trying to get even with evildoers by following their example.

Jesus Christ is the light of the world, and we also are the light of the world when we let the Christ light shine out through our thoughts and actions into the world, which so greatly needs spiritual light.

Think Godlike thoughts and you will become Godlike. In order that these good conditions may become permanent in your life and affairs, you must continually think and act in accordance with the divine plan, which includes the God attributes. "As he thinketh within himself, so is he."

Let your every act be tempered by your faith in God's unchanging goodness, manifesting through you. Let your every thought be in harmony with the divine plan. Thoughts of sin, sickness, weakness, anger, lust, jealousy, greed, fear, and death are not in harmony with the divine plan. Thoughts of righteousness, health, strength, love, life, and wisdom are in harmony with the divine plan.

When you think or act in one or more of the ways that are not in harmony with the divine plan, you get results in your life that are not good. You can change these conditions by changing your thinking. Here is the secret—think in harmony with the divine plan.

How to Overcome Your Enemies

Your enemies are not really people. Enemies are the wrong or dark thoughts that people think. Human enemies are in a sense the outpicturing of the dark thoughts that you and I and everyone else are thinking. When we erase these dark thoughts from our mind, we take the first step in overcoming our enemies.

The best way to dispel these dark thoughts is to bring the light of Christ into our consciousness. Christ will show us how to overcome our enemies with love. The light of Christ love can fill our being so full of powerful thoughts of Truth and light that there will be no room for enemy thoughts in us.

God did not create evil, and therefore evil thoughts are not real in His sight. They are real only in the realm of imagination in man's human thinking. God created good ideas only, and His good ideas are all-powerful. We, His children, are free to use His all-powerful ideas to overcome peacefully the weak, enemy thoughts of the world. Here are the names of some of our enemies that make our lives unhappy and full of strife: hate, fear, jealousy, ill will, selfishness, personal pride, greed, lust, suspicion, condemnation, revenge, worry, doubt, envy, and discouragement. All these conditions arise out of dark, negative thoughts that exist only in the minds of men. They will disappear when we realize that we are all-powerful children of God and fill our minds with the Christ light. Light always overcomes darkness and error.

According to Genesis 1:3, God created light on the first day, and we know that God's light is the spiritual foundation of our universe.

Enemy thoughts are the ugly, destructive products of man's wrong use of his power to think. God's creations are harmonious and constructive. Our fighting evil cannot overcome it, but when we turn on the light of Truth and harmony, evil will disappear.

Perfect love overcomes fear, hate, and other dark, inharmonious thoughts that are the cause of our unhappiness and insecurity. Security and true joy are parts of God's harmonious plan for us. We can accept His plan, which is His will for us, and enjoy His security and joy, or we can refuse to abide in His will and suffer from the unreality of darkness.

"The joy of Jehovah is your strength." Jesus Christ tried to show us how to overcome our enemies by using God's good ideas instead of man's destructive ideas. In the Book of Matthew, Jesus shows us how powerful love can be in helping us to overcome our enemies. This is what He says: "Ye have heard that it was said, Thou shalt love thy neighbor, and hate thine enemy; but I say unto you, Love your enemies, and pray for them that persecute you; that ye may be sons of your Father who is in heaven: for he maketh his sun to rise on the evil and the good, and sendeth rain on the just and the unjust. For if ye love them that love you, what reward have ye? do not even the publicans the same?" In Luke He says: "But love your enemies, and do *them* good, and lend, never despairing; and your reward shall be great, and ye shall be sons of the Most High; for he is kind toward the unthankful and evil. Be ye merciful, even as your Father is merciful. And judge not, and ye shall not be judged: and condemn not, and ye shall not be condemned: release, and ye shall be released: give, and it shall be given unto you; good measure, pressed down, shaken together, running over, shall they give unto your bosom. For with what measure ye mete it shall be measured to you again."

The destruction of our enemies, therefore, must begin in us, for when we are armed with Truth and act in accordance with God's thoughts, we can overcome the enemies in our own thoughts. Through the realization of God's light and Truth, we shall become so powerful that the enemy thoughts of other persons cannot harm us. We shall have power to find the Christ in others, and when we do this, we shall no longer need to fear or hate those who are suffering from their own dark thoughts.

We cannot destroy our enemies by warring upon and killing the men who are expressing the enemy thoughts. When we turn on the light of Christ in ourselves, we outshine the untrue thoughts of our supposed enemies, and as our light shines it reveals to us the good in the lives of others. We can best help those who seem to be our enemies by helping them to let their light shine and so reveal to themselves the nothingness of their enmity toward us.

The true light of Christ abides in everyone, but in many it is hidden under the bushel of their human ignorance and lack of spiritual understanding. The world needs more people who are willing to be illumined with the Christ light and who will radiate His love and harmony to others. Peace will come into manifestation internationally when more people become more interested in expressing God's love than they are in counting their enemies.

We can say that we believe in Christ but unless we think and radiate Christ thoughts and help others to think them, we cannot bring peace into our world. We cannot do away with war by fighting those who are war-minded. We must come out of the darkness of worldly thoughts of hate, fear, and strife by increasing the activity of our mind in thinking peaceful, loving thoughts. The power that holds God's creation in place and keeps it in harmonious activity is hidden in God's powerful ideas of love, harmony, freedom, life, forgiveness, unselfishness, and good judgment.

We must learn to agree with all the members of our family, in Christ, and when we do this, our whole family will be at peace in Spirit and in Truth. Then we shall find that the kingdom of God is truly with us in our household.

To be truly harmonious in our daily living we should let our love for God come first and our love for the members of our family come second. If we attach more importance to the members of our family than we do to God, they become to us, in a sense, enemies to true harmony in our home. It is written: "Even so, let your light shine before men; that they may see your good works, and glorify your Father who is in heaven." Let your Christ light shine before your family, and in so doing you will find the key that will open the door to peace and harmony for all its members.

When we let the true light of God shine in us, it will make our path so bright that no shadows will appear on it. Jesus Christ seemed to have enemies but He overcame them all. He even overcame death, the last enemy, because He would not give in to fear or contend with those who would kill Him. We, too, can overcome all enemies by following His example and His teaching.

The Last Straw

Quoting a popular saying is a poor excuse for indulging in a fit of rage or self-pity. To say, "That was the last straw" does not give one a right to act like a spoiled child.

"The last straw breaks the camel's back." That last straw has for hundreds of years been encouraging people to believe that they are justified in allowing some comparatively trivial matter to overrule their better judgment.

Of course there are times when a straw may not seem to be so trivial. It may look like a telephone pole, but that is because you are holding it too close to your eyes. Give it the proper perspective and it will be only a straw, and even though the old saying avers that it was that one little straw that broke the poor old camel's back, no one really believes that one straw could do such a thing.

Suppose you have done a great deal for someone, spent years of your time and lots of money on him, and then you find that he does not seem to appreciate what you have done. That may seem to be a pretty big straw, but remember that the weight of it depends upon your own thoughts about it. You can make it an overwhelming burden if you load it with depressing thoughts, regrets, sadness, and resentment, or you can make it as light as a feather by turning it quietly over to the Lord, who will gladly relieve you of its burden. The good you did, the service you rendered during the years, this was your means of expression. They were good for you. Bless them; bless what you did. Do not spoil it all now by condemning your good works.

Your reward comes from God. Keep sweet and enjoy your opportunity for serving. Your reward not only will come, but it has been coming to you from the Lord. He is blessing you now, but if you make burdens out of straws, you will fail to understand how He is trying to help you. If the person you helped does not appreciate what you did for him, do not make the same mistake and fail to appreciate the wonderful things God has been doing for you all these years.

You were created for the purpose of expressing

God's life, love, wisdom, and power. Doing things for others affords you an opportunity of living and enjoying life. If you could not render anyone a service, you would be unhappy indeed.

There is much remuneration in the joy of rendering a service, and additional remuneration will come to you according to the law of giving and receiving. If you are doing a kindness for the sake of a reward, for the sake of someone's appreciation, then are you not doing it for a selfish purpose instead of for the love of serving?

The last straw can be handled in several ways. It need not be still further weighted down with your leaden feelings of sorrow and weeping. It can be placed lightly on the top of the pile of service and its weight will never be noticed.

But look at your problem in another way. Let us consider that there is always a reason for everything that happens. If there is lack of appreciation, there is a reason for it. In order to bring appreciation from anyone, you must render something more than ordinary service. If a person works hard to please someone else and does it selfishly, he fails to stir up the true spirit of appreciation.

The "last straw" may in reality be only the straw that shows which way the wind blows. It may indicate that you have been looking to man for your reward instead of to God, and it may be a warning to you to change your attitude toward service.

The "last straw" breaks our camel's back only when we add the weight of our resistant attitude to it. God lightens all burdens. Jesus Christ gave the assurance that His yoke is easy and His burden is light, and He also said: "Whosoever would be first among you shall be your servant." The best way to make the last straw light is to bless it and thank God for it. If we can really rejoice when we bless the last straw, we shall be directed to a blessing. Then good must come from it to us even though we seemingly have depleted our earthly store in the service we have given.

By giving thanks to God, we open the floodgates of God's supply that will replenish our store. Remember that the last straw is very light and need not harm the camel at all.

Today many people are keeping themselves from entering into the blessings that might be theirs by complaining, by lacking faith, and by dwelling in the past. Everyone who desires to go forward and accomplish greater things must expect to find new and untried experiences in his path. New experiences and new problems indicate growth and progress. If we are able to master a new condition, we are then ready for still another experience. If we would progress toward the promised land we cannot expect to sit still and eat from the fleshpots of Egypt. We must go on into new thoughts and experiences. Some of these thoughts and experiences may seem to be lacking in interest and some may frighten us, but we must go steadily forward in the faith and assurance that God is guiding and caring for us. When we take this attitude, every adverse experience will be overcome as it makes its appearance. We shall not be frightened by any circumstance that may loom before us in the future. God will take care of every problem when it presents itself. Let us not borrow trouble from tomorrow. Let us not turn back or be afraid. Let us not lose faith. The race is not to the swift but to the one who endures with staunch faith to the end.

The Christ in me greets the Christ in you.

A Prayer Drill

First Day. *As I practice loving God with all my heart, soul, and strength, I am better able to see Him in other persons.*

Second Day. *Seeing the Christ in other persons helps me to become stronger in Christ, and it also helps them to find Christ in themselves.*

Third Day. *Because a man becomes like that which he sees with his mind's eye, I am resolved to practice seeing Christ in all persons, that I may become more Christlike.*

Fourth Day. *In Spirit and in Truth all men spring from God's perfect-man idea. We all therefore live, move, and have our being in God, and there is no cause for disagreement among us.*

Fifth Day. *My neighbor is Christ, who lives in even "the least of these." When I am kind to anyone, I am kind to Christ.*

Sixth Day. *My worldly affairs become orderly and harmonious as I cooperate with Christ in all persons with whom I have dealings.*

Seventh Day. *Because all people are members of the spiritual body of Christ, I serve Him best when I work together with others in love and harmony.*

Chapter 14

The Lord's Prayer

**I am open to the Father within
and I receive His love.**

Our Father

THIS very day you may exercise a most wonderful privilege which, if you avail yourself of it, will transform your life.

This privilege is yours no matter what mistakes you may have made in the past. It is this: You have the privilege now, this very moment, of making a new start by turning away from your old limiting thoughts and ideas, and accepting the idea that you are a child of God, the Father Almighty. This privilege, when accepted by you, will make you aware of your true heritage as a beloved child of God. You can accept this wonderful gift of God by turning to Him in Spirit, and speaking to Him as you would to your earthly father. When you can do this believing that He is your Father in heaven and that He hears you, you will feel His presence with you and within you, and you will know that He is truly your

Father. He is a loving Father who recognizes His
children and welcomes them gladly when they turn
to Him in love and faith and humility.

Everyone has a divine or Christ Self within him,
but most of us ignore this Self and thus fail to recognize ourselves as children of God. Jesus has
shown us how to approach the Father in Spirit and
in Truth, and to say in prayer, "Our Father who art
in heaven." When we do this in the name of the
perfect Christ Self that is within each one of us, we
shall know indeed that we are God's beloved children and that we are brothers and sisters of Jesus
Christ.

God is always present with us, but until we learn
to rise above our earthly problems and turn our
attention to Him in loving faith, we cannot understand how He is our true Father. When we do
become aware of our divine sonship, we are born
again, and we become spiritual brothers and sisters
of Jesus Christ.

Jesus explained that God must be worshiped in
Spirit and in Truth. This means that we must find
Him in our own inner temple and meet Him in
the secret place of the Most High. Here in quietness
and confidence we still all our tumultuous thoughts
concerning outer interests and listen to His still
small voice. We do not need to go into a church,
synagogue, temple, sacred mountain, or forest to
meet our loving Father-God, for He is everywhere

present in Spirit, and He is with us always, waiting for us to turn to Him and acknowledge our divine sonship.

Jesus' parable of the prodigal son shows how we are like the prodigal son who went into a far country and spent his substance until he began to be in want. His lack symbolizes need of spiritual joy, health, courage, and peace, which we shall receive bountifully from our Father when we return to His house. His loving hands are stretched out to us, His son, who was lost but now has come to himself and returned to his Father.

We do not need to depend upon someone else to make intercession with the Father for us. However, others are helpful to us at times in directing our way, but each person must eventually meet the Father alone in his own inner Christ nature. Each one must find out for himself that God is his loving Father.

Our heavenly Father is easy to approach, and He will meet us partway as the father in the parable came out to meet the returning prodigal son. God is much more understanding of His children's needs than an earthly father can be. We cannot see Him with our physical eyes nor can we find Him in our material possessions, for He is Spirit. Also, we must speak to Him through our own inner spiritual thought. Spirit speaks to Spirit.

When our Spirit sincerely speaks to our heavenly

Father, then our whole being becomes illumined with His presence. No one is far from God, for He is everywhere present. But we shall find God in Spirit through our faith, love, and obedience as we search for Him with all our heart.

God loves us more than we can ever understand, but we can appreciate His love more as we love Him more. And when we love Him more, we shall also be loving other people more. We shall not confine our love to the members of our own family and a few friends, but we shall love everybody.

The next time we repeat the Lord's Prayer, let us think of ourselves as speaking earnestly to a Father who is more loving than our earthly father could be, and who is able to understand our every problem and to supply our every need. When we consciously become aware of our divine sonship, we are born again and are a new creature in Spirit.

We do not need to wait for some appointed time in the future to come into our divine sonship, for God is always here. Let us find Him and acknowledge Him as our Father today.

Who Art in Heaven

Heaven is a state of consciousness, not a place that you can know through your five physical senses. Heaven is not outside of you—it is within you, just as Jesus said it is.

"God's in his heaven—
All's right with the world!"

Do not the days and the seasons come and go in a regular order more lasting and dependable than any mechanism ever invented by man? This state of order has lasted from time immemorial. Does this not prove that all is right with the world? When you abide with God in His heavenly state of mind, all will be right in your world, and the affairs of your world will also move in divine order.

When we make room for God in our inner consciousness, we become consciously aware of the Truth that we are indeed a temple of the living God. When we speak to Him in the inner closet of our being, "the secret place of the Most High," He hears us. We do not need to shout at Him or to go through formal ceremonies to attract His attention. He hears us when we speak to Him silently in Spirit and in Truth. Outer forms and ceremonies are not a necessary part of our prayers when we realize that God is Spirit. Forms and ceremonies may help those persons who have not caught the spiritual vision of God's true nature by reminding them of their duty to pray regularly, but these outer forms are not necessary. When we ask sincerely with faith in the Spirit of our loving Father, He "who seeth in secret" will reward us openly, as Jesus promised.

We cannot see God any more than we can see love, but as we can see what love does through those persons who express it, we can also see the results of God's power in our world.

God is love, and when we love Him in Spirit and in Truth, He works in and through us. We cannot see Spirit, but we can perceive it and feel it with our inner faculties. We cannot see life, but we can feel it surging in us as we think, move about, and express ourselves in many ways. Christ in us is the door to God's kingdom, because Christ is the image and likeness of God. It is Christ who speaks God's language within us. When we become aware of our Christ Self, we are born again and we come into a new understanding of life.

Before we find Christ within us and are born again, we may feel that we are mere flesh-and-blood beings animated by a mysterious force called life. But when we become aware of the Christ Spirit within us, we realize that we are truly more than we appear to be, that we are spiritual beings dwelling in marvelously constructed bodies of flesh. We then become spiritually aware that in truth we are children of God.

God loves His children, and when they are willing to turn away for a time from their mad search for happiness and satisfaction in the glamour of the world, and seek for these gifts in His kingdom within themselves, He is always glad to converse with them. When they turn to God in love and faith, they will find Him waiting for them, and then they will realize that He is able and willing to help them find everything that they need to supply their temporal needs. The promise will be fulfilled: "Seek ye first his kingdom, and his righteousness; and all these things shall be added unto you."

God does not hide Himself from us, but it is we who hide from Him. We carelessly turn away from Him in our selfish pursuits for happiness and gain in the world. God is our nearest and dearest friend and counselor, who is always ready to help us.

When we are able to speak the words of the Lord's Prayer with spiritual faith and understanding we realize a new and deeper meaning in the following line, which we often repeat mechanically: "Thy kingdom come. Thy will be done in earth, as it is in heaven." We begin to realize that in this prayer we are asking for God's kingdom to come onto the earth and not that we may be taken up out of the earth into the heavens of God's kingdom in the faraway skies.

The earth is not evil. It is a proving ground where the spiritual kingdom of God may be made manifest. Man is the ruler of the world, and when he finds his true spiritual authority as a child of God, he will be able to bring God's kingdom into the world, where it will cause all things to shine with a new beauty that he has never seen there before.

The earth is just a material world to us until we discover that God's Spirit permeates all things. This knowledge comes to us when we have found the Christ in ourselves. Then we shall be able to behold a new heaven and a new earth within us and all about us. All the world about us will then be filled with life, love, joy, and peace, where before we have seen only a cold, material world with a distant heaven hanging above it. We shall have discovered that heaven is at hand, that God is everywhere present, and that the earth is full of Him and His goodness.

We must discover this Truth about God's omnipresent glory in Spirit before we can enter into its perfection. God is in the world, and His goodness and beauty are everywhere present in Spirit in everything. Men must first discover God in their hearts before they can find Him in outer things.

Hallowed Be Thy Name

God's true name is so wonderful that it cannot be written in English, Hebrew, Aramaic, Latin, or Greek characters, nor can it be spoken by human tongue, for God is Spirit, and Spirit cannot be adequately described in earthly terms.

Our English word *God* is a word that we have agreed upon to designate the great living One, who created the world and all things in it, including man. This mighty, living One, who cares for all of

His creation and guides the courses of the planets, is like a loving earthly father.

If we should like to learn more about the true name of our wonderful, loving, heavenly Father, we must search for and know Him in Spirit, and not be content to know Him only by the name that we have given Him. To learn His true name we must explore the realm in which our Father, the Supreme Being, dwells, which lies deeper than the objective surface of matter. We can begin to do this by practicing in our inner life some of His spiritual attributes, an important one of which is love.

Love is the name we have given to a spiritual power, but this name means nothing to a person who does not actually feel the power of love in his own heart. The more deeply we feel love, the more we are able to understand what love is. We can never learn to understand very much about love as a power by studying and analyzing only its superficial name, "love."

God's true name is a living power, not a printed group of letters. It is luminous, powerful, everywhere present, loving, and wise. It is hallowed, because it is always a blessing and it is full of righteousness, harmony, and order. I am not trying to depreciate the value of the man-made word *God,* as we use it, because it is a signal to us to search deeper and find in Spirit what this word truly represents.

This little word is a sign that can point the way

inward into the realm of Spirit, where we shall be able to gain a more perfect understanding of the divine nature of love. When we call upon God, our Father, and use the name "God" with faith, earnestness, and meekness, we establish a degree of contact with the divine consciousness of God's true name, even though it is beyond our intellectual comprehension.

Even though the name "God" is inadequate to describe our Father, it becomes more wonderful to us as we look beyond it and are able to behold the true name, which cannot be written on the pages of books. The name "God" can become a connecting link between man's understanding and his Father's hallowed name when man wills it so.

Our Father's name is hallowed because it is powerful to do good, to guide, to heal, and to prosper those who seek in the realm of their highest and best thoughts for a glimpse of His majesty and magnificence.

We can approach His name in Spirit and in understanding through prayer, but we cannot approach His name so long as our minds are filled with petty, deceitful, selfish, jealous, hateful, negative thoughts, which prevent us from praying. When we put aside selfish little personal thoughts and replace them with love, forgiveness, and praise, a better understanding of His name will be revealed to us, and we shall enter into a larger and happier view of life.

When we know the name of our Father, the Divine Being, it will radiate to us righteousness, love, harmony, and all that is good as we seek it and find it in Spirit and in Truth. As we abide in His name, we are filled with courage, peace, understanding, power, love, and harmony. Our health improves, our joy increases, and our prosperity becomes manifest in greater measure. As we call upon our Father in our deeper understanding of His name, we become quickened by His Spirit and are transformed into the likeness of the Christ. Let us therefore, when we repeat this part of the Lord's Prayer, "Hallowed be thy name," think more deeply and sincerely about the divine potentialities that are contained in that hallowed name.

Thy Kingdom Come

The kingdom of God is a spiritual state, and does not occupy space as do the kingdoms of the earth.

Jesus told the Pharisees that the kingdom of God is not a worldly kingdom. He explained this by saying that the kingdom of God does not come by observation, but rather it is within each individual. The kingdom of God is a spiritual estate. Because God is Spirit, He does not need to sit upon a material throne.

God is everywhere present. Therefore His kingdom must also be everywhere present. We find the kingdom of God in the innermost part of our own being, just as we find our thoughts within ourself. Thoughts do not occupy space, because they are not dimensional. Our thoughts may be concerned with material things, and when we put these thoughts into action, material things are changed to agree with their mental or spiritual counterpart.

If you allow God's Truth to direct your words and actions, you become a channel through which the power of the kingdom works to make perfect your life and affairs. You cannot see thoughts; neither can you see the kingdom of God. This spiritual kingdom does not come with observation, for it can be found only within you. This is true even though the kingdom of God is everywhere present. Your own heart is your place of contact with the kingdom of God.

Your mind is the connecting link between you and God's kingdom. When you find the kingdom of God within yourself, you will then be able to recognize it in other persons. When you consciously abide in the kingdom, you will be able to look out into the material world with a new spiritual vision that reveals that the heavenly state pervades everything. Thus will the kingdom of God come onto the earth through you.

Jesus did not think of the kingdom of God as being located in some distant place or state in a future time, for He said: "Verily I say unto you,

There are some of them that stand here, who shall in no wise taste of death, till they see the Son of man coming in his kingdom." Jesus, at another time, said: "The time is fulfilled, and the kingdom of God is at hand: repent ye, and believe in the gospel." And He also said to His disciples: "And as ye go, preach, saying, The kingdom of heaven is at hand."

Jesus thought of the kingdom as a spiritual place, for He said to the Samaritan woman at the well: "But the hour cometh, and now is, when the true worshippers shall worship the Father in spirit and truth: for such doth the Father seek to be his worshippers. God is spirit: and they that worship him must worship in spirit and truth."

Neither can we enter into the kingdom by merely speaking to God with our lips. We must go deeper into our heart where we can indeed become one with God through the Christ Spirit in us. Jesus said: "Not every one that saith unto me, Lord, Lord, shall enter into the kingdom of heaven; but he that doeth the will of my Father who is in heaven."

To do the will of the Father is to practice love and forgiveness for our neighbors. We must love righteousness more than we love to have our own way. If we say, "Peace, peace," and still have in our heart a stubborn desire to promote our own personal will, we cannot have peace, nor can we enter into the kingdom of God.

Our human personality often plays tricks on us. We may desire to enter into the kingdom of God and enjoy its peace and harmony while we are still determined to have our own way. Sometimes in a subtle way we try to convince ourselves that we are right when in our heart we know we are wrong. We may have taken a certain stand in some discussion in the past, perhaps a very unimportant matter, and we are now adamant in maintaining our position, even after we can see that we were wrong. We now seek to justify ourselves with arguments and excuses as we try to prove to ourselves and others that we are right. In this state of mind we cannot enter into the kingdom of God.

If we would enter the kingdom where peace, righteousness, and happiness are the reality, we must be willing to admit we are wrong and humbly ask forgiveness when we see our error. The personal self must become very meek before it can enter into the kingdom of God. Self-justification never brought heavenly peace to anyone.

When you are working with others, you can keep your peace by promoting agreement rather than disagreement in the group. Jesus said: "Again I say unto you, that if two of you shall agree on earth as touching anything that they shall ask, it shall be done for them of my Father who is in heaven."

No good and lasting thing can be accomplished through disagreement. The great need in the world today is for agreement and unity of purpose in the family, in politics, in the church, and among nations. Heaven is a state of peace and harmony among men.

Thy Will Be Done

The best use that any man can make of his willpower is to will that God's will be done in him and in his affairs.

This is the wisest, most practical, and rewarding use any person can make of his willpower, because God's will is good. Therefore, it can bring only good to the man who expresses God's goodwill freely. When a man allows God's good will to radiate through him to his fellowmen, he finds that he draws to himself rich rewards that he could not receive by using his own will, unaided by God's will.

Expressing God's will toward our fellowmen in sincerity and truth means more than merely smiling at people and being generous and pleasant to them. Sincerely expressing goodwill toward our fellowmen will lead us to a deeper understanding of God's will for us, which includes healing, harmony, prosperity, guidance, love, forgiveness, and happiness. We find that all good things are included in God's will for us. We cannot freely express God's will and at the same time remain in ruts of worry, sadness, self-pity, or insufficiency.

Jesus did the will of God, and through its power He was able to bless and heal many people. He once said: "I seek not mine own will, but the will of Him that sent me." He invited His followers to share divine sonship with Him when He said: "For whosoever shall do the will of my Father who is in heaven, he is my brother, and sister, and mother." He promised many wonderful things for all God's children when He said: "For the Father loveth the Son, and showeth him all things that himself doeth: and greater works than these will he show him."

When we follow our own selfish will and refuse to be led by God's good, wise will, we are likely to meet with difficulties that we could have avoided. If we work closely with God's will, we shall be spared many troubles, misunderstandings, and mistakes.

In His parable of the self-made man who thought more of his own will than he did of God's loving will, Jesus gave an example of the futility of the efforts of the personal will. In Luke 12:18, 19 (ASV), we find this worldly-minded man reasoning as follows: "This will I do: I will pull down my barns, and build greater; and there will I bestow all my grain and my goods. And I will say to my soul, Soul, thou hast much goods laid up for many years; take thine ease, eat, drink, be merry." But because he followed his own will instead of the divine will, he lost contact with God's life. He also lost his ability to enjoy these material things which he had stored up, and they were no longer useful to him.

By following God's will, we store up our riches in heaven where they are not taken away from us. These riches which are stored in heaven within us include life, love, happiness, wisdom, and peace. As we follow God's will and seek the kingdom of heaven first, all of the other things we need are added to us.

When we follow God's will, we are able to enjoy all things that come into our life experience. Material things become less important and will be supplied by the loving Father when we allow His Spirit to work in and through us. All good things have been prepared for us and are waiting in abundance, but by following our selfish will, we often turn away from them as the prodigal son did. But when the prodigal son finally realized his mistake and saw that he would be better off as a servant in his father's house, he was wise enough to change his mind and return to his father. He said: "I will arise and go to my father."

When we, like the prodigal son, come to ourselves and realize that our Father-God is truly the source of our good and return to Him in humility, His loving-kindness will come to meet us and bless us.

We should never fear that God's will for us may bring sorrow or punishment to us. God's will being done in us can remove from our lives some of the barriers that seem to be standing between us and our true happiness and peace. But in the end we shall be greatly blessed, because we shall see that all things in our life are working together for good, even those things which seemed at first to be evil.

What Jesus said concerning little children applies to all of His children. "Even so it is not the will of your Father who is in heaven, that one of these little ones should perish."

In Earth as It Is in Heaven

You are a spiritual being living in a so-called material world. This world is more wonderful than it appears to be to your physical eyes, for it is alive with God life.

We cannot see this life, but we can see the result of its expression in every growing plant, tree, and living creature. The world about us is like a mirror in that it reflects what we think and feel, and sends back to us in our daily experiences what we are thinking about. For example, when we think of and feel God's love, our loving state of mind is reflected back to us in the loving deeds of persons, and in harmonious experiences in the daily routine of living. When we feel the spirit of God's love in our heart, we are able to see more of His beauty and goodness in the persons we meet and in the material objects that come into our field of experience.

Through His loving word God has created all things, including this manifest world. It too must be good, because all God's creations are good.

When we look out upon the world about us with God's love warming our heart, our eyes and senses are quickened by His power and we begin to see more of His goodness in all things.

If we could see the world as God sees it, we should behold a good world, for God is of "purer eyes than to behold evil." When we keep the eye of our consciousness single to the good, we see only God's good creation; but when we permit it to wander away from Him as eternal Good, we "see double," that is, we see both good and evil.

Thinking un-Godlike thoughts causes us to look at God's good world through the dark glass of our own foggy thinking. This doubtful state of mind bogs us down in doubt, uncertainty, worry, and inharmony. When we seem to be helplessly lost in the troubles of our world, which, strangely enough, we ourselves have created by our own negative thinking, we see trouble and discord about us, when we should see goodness and harmony. When this condition exists, it indicates that we need to clean house. We need a cleansing flood of Spirit to come into our being and wash our mind and heart clean of muddy thoughts.

This cleansing process, which causes old things to pass away, is not always pleasant to experience while it is taking place, but it clears the way for new joy and peace to come to us. Noah's flood is a symbol of this experience taking place in our mind and affairs, and we shall come out cleansed and renewed if we sincerely hold to our faith in God's omnipresent power and goodness. We must keep our faces turned toward the one God and His everlasting goodness, while we resolutely turn away from the lesser gods of our own creation. These are the gods of strife, greed, lust, jealousy, fear, selfishness, and hatred. They are idols of man's making. Thus, with singleness of purpose we invoke the baptism of the Holy Spirit to wash away the errors of our past.

To make room in our life for new blessings that God has prepared for us, our inner consciousness must be baptized by the Holy Spirit. This baptism must take place before the old memories of error thoughts and conditions can be washed away from it. After our consciousness has been cleansed of the old memories of error thoughts and conditions, the good memories that we have saved in our Ark will come forth and multiply in our life and affairs, and will supply all our needs both spiritual and physical. With a clean slate we begin to live anew and to prove the wonders of the power of God's love working in and through us.

In God's heaven all is good and harmonious. We can find His heaven within us by seeking it with our whole heart, soul, mind, and strength, and when we do find it, the earth on which we live will then become to us like the heaven that is within us.

While on the earth we are really in the school of

life learning how to become perfect, like our Father in heaven, and how better to appreciate His spiritual riches.

God is with us in Spirit at all times, but we must learn how to find Him and work with Him. He will help us when we will let Him. He has given us freedom to think and to do as we please, for freedom is a part of His goodness. Without freedom we could never develop our inner strength and understanding and become a willing and cooperative member of His household. We have the opportunity to try to prove all things so that we can hold fast to that which is good. Paul tells us to "prove all things; hold fast that which is good."

When we exercise our freedom of thinking, we discover for ourselves how to discard the tares of negative thoughts and harvest the wheat of right thoughts. Thus, with understanding and appreciation we shall be able to gather the fruits of God's love and dwell in the kingdom. We shall be able to dwell in the kingdom when we love to be in it better than anything else.

We are free to think what we choose to think, but we shall never be truly free from our own self-imposed bondage until we know God's Truth. "Ye shall know the truth, and the truth shall make you free." God has given us freedom, but we must prove that we are free by knowing and demonstrating what freedom means.

The truth is that God's kingdom must be brought onto the earth by man and that man can be free only when he loves God and his fellowmen with all his heart.

Give Us This Day Our Daily Bread

Daily bread means more than just bread made from grain. It represents God-substance. One manifest form of this substance is food.

Like love, life, and wisdom, substance is one of God's spiritual principles. God's principle of substance is the spiritual essence of all that exists. It is always present everywhere in abundance sufficient for all the needs of His vast creation.

God's principles cannot be diminished by man's use of them. But by using these principles rightly, man can bring about an increased expression of them in his life.

Omnipresent substance is always available for those who have faith in God's all-sufficiency. Manifestations of God's substance cannot be stored away and kept out of circulation by man for any great period of time, for God's substance is free and cannot therefore be restrained too long from its divine mission of serving mankind. It is true that many foods can be kept for a reasonable period of time by being artificially treated and preserved, but the God-substance manifested in them must eventually go back to work for God by appearing again and again in new forms.

God-substance, when it is manifested as food, is continually being expressed in new forms through the process of change and growth. Even this substance of our body is being continuously renewed. A little bit of us dies every day, and our body is renewed and resurrected daily. This is God-life in action in us.

We can help the forces of renewal that are working in our body to keep ahead of the processes of deterioration and decay if we will renew our mind daily. What we believe in our mind is reflected in our body.

Our daily bread, which comes from God, includes food for our Spirit and mind as well as for our body. If we remember this and assimilate new ideas as well as food when we eat, we shall be renewed and healed in mind and body. God is sending us food each day for our threefold being.

We must forgive yesterday's mistakes and allow them to pass away from our mind, just as the worn-out cells are discarded from our body. We are renewed daily by the renewing of our mind with the help of Christ within us. We must forgive old thoughts and let them go freely to make room in our mind to receive new, fresh, life-giving, inspiring thoughts from God each day. We must let go of the old sorrows, disappointments, worries, and grudges of yesterday so that we may receive each day new inspiration from God's vital, living, joyous, peaceful, life-giving thoughts fresh from the fountain of His infinite supply.

We should not spoil our today's bread by worrying about the past or the future. We must live now as we appropriate our daily bread with our Spirit, mind, and body. Doubts concerning where tomorrow's supply of food is coming from always work against our best interests. We should bless the food we eat today and not curse it by thinking fear and worry thoughts.

When we worry about tomorrow's bread, we prove that we lack faith in God's supply. While we are worrying, we are unable to receive full nourishment from our food to satisfy all three departments of our being. We must live one day at a time, giving thanks each day that our food is coming to us fresh from the hand of God as we need it. Even the food that we may have temporarily stored away on our shelves is able to receive God's blessings and to bless us when we open the way by giving thanks for it.

By our thanks we set free the God-substance in the food so that it expands to meet our needs. It also enlarges our awareness of the God-substance for our food.

All three departments of our being must be fed. Feeding the body alone is not sufficient or satisfying. The mind of man hungers for joy, appreciation, harmony, and kindness, and his spirit hungers for God's Truth, life, and wisdom. Our daily bread, therefore, is not merely the material food we eat, but it also includes God's inspiration and loving-kindness.

Giving thanks daily to God opens the way for the true Spirit of substance to feed our spirit, as well as our mind and body. No matter through what channel our food may come to us, we should not forget that it originates as spiritual substance in God's creative Word, and that it can bring us greater life, strength, and inspiration when we eat it to the glory of God with thankfulness, love, joy, and peace of mind.

Remembering God's omnipresent goodness, we need never be fearful or worried concerning tomorrow's supply. Our faith and praise will keep the channel between us and God's inexhaustible source open.

Forgive Us Our Debts

God has given us everything that we possess. Though we owe Him for so much, He does not press us for payment, for He is our loving Father. Like a good earthly father, all that He requires of us is obedience and cooperation. He forgives us for everything, even our mistakes, when we are willing to accept His love and forgiveness by loving Him and forgiving our debtors.

The pattern of God's plan for us is love and forgiveness. To fit ourselves into this plan we must change our thought habits so that our thoughts will conform more closely to His thoughts. He has given us much of all that is good because He loves us, but in order for us to understand His love and forgiveness we must also practice loving and forgiving. Just as proof of the pudding is in the eating, so the proof of God's love is in our appropriating it.

The whole creation is built upon the firm foundation of God's love, which is the greatest power in the universe. Jesus reminds us that upon love hang "the whole law . . . and the prophets." Our life will become a harmonious factor in the working of God's law when we practice loving God and our fellowmen with all our heart, soul, and mind. Paul tells us, "Owe no man anything, save to love one another."

These words of Jesus and Paul seem to indicate that all law is founded upon love.

God's gifts to us include life, love, substance, power, harmony, understanding, beauty, free will, judgment, order, and many wonderful things that we have not yet discovered for ourselves. All these gifts become ours in fact to the extent that we learn how to use them rightly. As we love God more, we shall understand love better, and also His other gifts.

God does not demand of us payment for these

gifts, and yet in a way we are obligated to Him. We can pay our debt by working with Him continually in Spirit and in Truth.

As we love God more, we shall understand Him better. The scientist who loves his work learns more about the things he is studying than those who do not love the things that they are studying and working with. We also will understand our neighbor better when we love him more.

All the world today needs more love. If a majority of the people in any nation would express love toward God and man, they would become a balance that would help to steady all the other nations and keep them at peace.

Those who lack love are always afraid of something. When a person is afraid, he either runs away from his problems or fights against them. These actions are both wasteful and useless. A loving attitude will help to solve all problems.

Jesus teaches us to be perfect as our Father in heaven is perfect. We find the proof of God's perfection in His abiding love for His children and His ever-ready forgiveness of their many mistakes. But His love could mean so much more to us than it now means to the average man if we would work, think, and live more consciously with Him.

If we would practice expressing love, not just sentimental love but the true spirit of love, toward our neighbors and God, we should learn how to understand better and enjoy the wonderful gifts that God's love has placed in our hands and hearts.

These gifts are always here, ready for us to use, but when our attitude is negative because we lack love, we are blind to these good things. Electricity has always been here on earth; it was here long before men learned how to use it or were even aware of its presence, except as lightning. Benjamin Franklin, who sent his kite up into the sky during a storm in order to learn more about the properties of lightning, learned that an electric current would flow down his kite string. Others, who put their minds and hearts into the further study of electricity, have discovered many of its secrets and have made it possible for all men to benefit by its usefulness. And men are still discovering new electrical marvels every day.

So it is with the law of love. Love has always been here, but only a few people, comparatively speaking, have been able to use it in a practical way, because, unlike electricity, love must be discovered anew by every person who would benefit by its wonders. Electricity, when applied to laborsaving mechanical devices for the outer man's pleasure and comfort, is accepted and used by many persons who are slow to accept the practical application of love to their worldly affairs, even though Jesus Christ has made its application so clear. For the power of love to be effective in the life of an individual, he must discover it within himself in his own inner kingdom and apply it to all his affairs.

Wasteful wars are due to men's lack of understanding and appreciation of the great law of love. Because people do not accept and use this mighty power of love, they fearfully stoop to use destructive powers in an effort to save themselves from harm or loss. These destructive powers include worry, hatred, greed, selfishness, suspicion, and the like. When we employ love, we are aided by a host of its agents, which include understanding, goodwill, peace, harmony, and many other positive powers. These agents will help us to solve all of our difficult problems.

When we understand love better, we shall see that our problems are usually caused by fearful, negative attitudes that beset us when we do not have love to guide us. We would not have wars if we would appreciate God's love enough to return a little of it to Him and to our fellowmen to repay Him for His loving-kindness.

We can pay all our debts, both to man and God, by expressing our love and forgiveness toward God and man. If we owe somebody money, love will not let us withhold payment, but it will show us ways in which we can earn the money necessary to pay the debt. We can pay all debts, as well as our great debt to our Father-God, by loving Him and forgiving ourselves and our fellowmen, even though some persons may not seem to appreciate our love at first. Our Father-God goes on loving us and forgiving us, even though some of us refuse to appreciate His efforts.

The person who is forgiving always enjoys a peaceful, happy state of mind. The one who does not forgive, even though he is forgiven by God and man, is usually in an unhappy, disturbed state of mind.

God forgives us all our debts every day, and when we are able to appreciate what this means and begin to love Him in return, and to practice forgiveness ourselves, we shall be able to receive and enjoy the full benefits of His wonderful, forgiving love in our life.

We Forgive Our Debtors

The power to forgive is like a magic key that we can use to unlock and release the chains forged by negative thoughts with which we have bound ourselves.

Thoughts and feelings of criticism, misunderstanding, hatred, doubt, fear, jealousy, resentment, selfishness, and the like are the chains that bind us and prevent us from freely expressing the divine powers that have been given us by our heavenly Father.

God does not punish us when we bind ourselves

by thinking negative thoughts, for He loves us and wants to help us to be free, happy, and prosperous. Because He loves us, He has given us this wonderful key, the power to forgive, so that we may free ourselves from our own devices. We should, therefore, continually give thanks to God for this wonderful key, which can aid us every day to free ourselves from the bondage of our negative thinking.

Nearly every day we bind ourselves by making the mistake of thinking limiting thoughts about other persons and conditions that we do not like. However, when we use our magic key and forgive our debtors and our offenders, we set ourselves free and are ready to take another step toward attaining our divine inheritance as perfect children of God.

We cannot attempt to bind other persons without binding ourselves. When we forgive those whom we have considered to be our debtors, we are forgiven and released from the chains that we forged by our limited thinking. If we want others to forgive us, we must first forgive them.

Our thoughts are creative and build into our life the kind of things we think about. By our past thoughts and actions we have drawn to us the kind of things that we are now enjoying or grumbling about. If we are unhappy, we may think that other persons are to blame for our present unhappiness, but we should remember that in Truth we are all one in Spirit and therefore whatsoever we do to others or think about others, according to God's law, is being done to us.

Jesus tells us that whatever we do unto *"even these least"* we do unto Him. When we are loving and kind to another person, we glorify the Christ in ourselves. When we are unkind and hateful to another person, we deny the Christ in ourselves.

God's law is perfect and good. When we work with it, we are blessed, but when we work contrary to it, we bruise ourselves on the rough places of our own creation. What we do unto others, the law of cause and effect will return to us. When we break the law, we bring punishment upon ourselves; it is not our loving Father-God who punishes us.

When we bless, we are blessed; when we criticize, we are criticized; when we give, we receive; when we forgive, we are forgiven; and when we fight, we stir up antagonism against ourselves. The Truth is that we ourselves decide whether we shall be free or bound.

God's law will bring freedom to all who observe it. If we use our freedom to bind others, we shall be bound, because we are disobeying the law. If we try to enslave others, even in our imagination, we become enslaved. If we set others free and bless them, we are freed and blessed. Our loving, freeing thoughts clear the way for the light of Truth to shine into our lives and reveal the Truth to us in greater degree.

Do not make the mistake of thinking you can condemn others without bringing condemnation upon yourself. This reaction is illustrated every day in the lives of many people. It is especially noticeable in daily news reports that recite the confusion in our political affairs. It seems that those who are most critical receive the most criticism. The world needs more words of praise, Truth, righteousness, love, and thankfulness, and a forgiving attitude.

A positive and constructive attitude is the answer to all the problems of life. Let us not stand on the negative side of life, but let us stand firmly and joyously on the positive, constructive side with God. If we are already bound by the negation we have stirred up, let us begin to free ourselves this minute by using the key of forgiveness, both for others and for ourselves.

After we forgive, we can exercise and enjoy our freedom still more by sending out love, goodwill, praise, and thankfulness toward God and all persons everywhere.

Leave Us Not in Temptation

Remember that God is our loving Father. It is hard to believe that He would lead His children into temptation. It would seem therefore more fitting for us to say when we pray to Him, "Leave us not in temptation," or, "Abandon us not in temptation," instead of saying, "Lead us not into temptation."

Because God loves us so much, He is always with us, but how can we enjoy His presence unless we are friendly toward Him and talk to Him often? We must become aware of His presence before we can receive His instructions. We can become aware of His presence by loving Him and having faith in Him.

When we are being tempted by our selfish human desires, we should seek God and remember that He is with us and will help us to overcome our temptations. It is unthinkable that we should need to pray to God not to lead us into temptation.

God wants us to be free to think and to do as we choose, but He always rejoices when we choose to call upon Him to help us to overcome the temptation that our freedom permits us to conceive in our own mind. The temptations that we encounter grow out of our ignorance and willfulness. With God's help we grow stronger and wiser by overcoming these temptations.

God rejoices when we use the will and the freedom He has given us to overcome temptations. As we pray, we gain understanding and become stronger through exercising our God-given powers righteously. And as we grow stronger and wiser, we become more like the perfect Son, who is Christ in us.

God loves us so much that He wants us to prove

and understand better the meaning of our divine sonship and become consciously aware of His loving Fatherhood. When we become wise enough and strong enough to do what is right and to use wisely the powers that He has given us, we shall be able to sit down at the right hand of His throne with Jesus Christ.

An earthly father loves his child and is sorry when the child hurts himself by falling when he first tries to walk, but the understanding father knows that the child is learning by these falls. He therefore does not punish the child for trying, but encourages him to try again and again. He knows that the child must learn to walk and he rejoices when the child makes the effort even though he may fall down and bump his nose.

The father could prevent the child from experiencing some bumps by carrying him in his arms, but he knows that if he does not allow the little one to try for himself he will never learn to walk. While he is learning, the child must be free to try to walk, even though he falls at times. The child's muscles will grow strong only when he uses them.

The earthly father does not want his child to hurt himself, but he does want him to learn how to walk. Neither does our heavenly Father want us to hurt ourselves when we are learning to walk in His way. He does not put obstacles in our path, but He actually makes the way smooth for us.

Nevertheless, we must prove ourselves and cultivate our spiritual abilities before we can walk with God in His way. While learning, we may make mistakes and fall down many times. These mistakes we may call sins, but the Father is always present, ready to forgive, encourage, and help us when we will listen to His guidance.

If we hold onto God's hand and trust in Him at all times, even when we make mistakes that cause us to fall, He will guide us along the path, and we shall grow spiritually strong as we learn to walk in His way.

Through learning how to do the Father's will, even by hard experiences and mistakes, we become stronger spiritually, and better able to work understandingly with our heavenly Father.

We can prove our appreciation for God's love and all His other spiritual gifts by walking with Him and conversing with Him daily. Thus we can use our freedom to glorify Him instead of misusing it to fall into temptation.

We can turn temptation into profitable lessons that will bring us victory if we will have faith in God's help. If we learn nothing from our mistake, we lose by it, but if we learn how to do better next time, we gain.

By looking steadfastly to God we seldom make serious mistakes, for He gives us the power of love and wisdom to meet all our problems in the world.

We do not need to travel through life by the hard way of ignorance and woe, for we can begin now by the help of God's guidance to profit by our past mistakes and not repeat them.

As we keep our eyes fixed upon God, the light of His countenance will guide us into the right way so that we shall become master of our life as Jesus Christ, our Elder Brother, demonstrated. He has shown us the way, which is the way of faith.

When we pray, "Leave us not in temptation," we prove that we have faith in God's love for us, and that we are not afraid that He may send temptations upon us. God is Spirit, and He is perfect love. We must learn to look to Him for love and guidance and not for punishment.

When we walk in His way, we behold the beauties of His handiwork everywhere and rejoice; and we are courageous, understanding, loving, and kind.

But Deliver Us from Evil

Evil is not a real power. It is only a negative condition that appears in the affairs of the manifest world, and it is caused by man's failure to understand and apply the only true power, which is the power of God's love.

When we think of evil as a power opposing God's true power, we are ascribing a semblance of power to a condition that is brought about by man's failure to believe in and apply the true power of God's love. The only power that evil can have over us is the power that we give it by our thoughts.

We make a great mistake when we try to destroy evil by using physical means, or by fighting it. Jesus taught us that evil cannot be overcome by evil, but that it can be overcome only by good. Good is a positive power. Good is like light, which is the only thing that can overcome darkness. This proves that darkness is nothing more than the absence of light.

We cannot banish darkness by trying to drive it out by force, nor can we dispel it by adding more darkness to it. To try to overcome evil with evil would be like trying to dispel darkness by adding more darkness to what you already have. Only light can overcome darkness, because darkness is just the absence of light. Bring the light in, and darkness disappears.

There is no darkness so powerful that it can extinguish the light of even one little candle. So it is with good. Evil cannot destroy the goodness of a kind deed, no matter how insignificant the deed might be. What we call evil is often merely man's lack of ability to express goodness.

God is the source of all goodness, and when we do not try to understand God, we fail to reach the mark of His goodness. We call this failure sin. The only way we can overcome our sin of missing the mark of "the high calling of God in Christ Jesus" is to perfect our ability to think straight and keep our eye single to the mark of God's perfection. We cannot serve two masters. We cannot believe both in God and in Satan.

When we think of evil as a real power, we are setting up in our mind a belief in a power that is opposed to God. When we believe in Satan we are trying to believe in two gods, a good and a bad god. But God has said: "Thou shalt have no other gods before me."

Realizing the Truth there is only one God and that He is a good God will set us free from the power of evil.

In the Lord's Prayer we ask God to deliver us from evil. The only way we can be delivered from evil is for us to follow the first and greatest commandment. We must love God with all our mind and strength, and stop using our mind and strength to fight evil as though it were a thing having power.

The first and greatest commandment is: "Thou shalt love the Lord thy God with all thy heart, and with all thy soul, and with all thy strength, and with all thy mind." When we love God in this way, we shall fill our heart and mind so full of the light of love that there will be no dark place in us where thoughts of evil can hide. Our whole body will be full of light if we keep our eye single to the light.

Jesus said: "I am come a light into the world, that whosoever believeth on me may not abide in the darkness." He also reminded us that the light came into the world and men loved the darkness rather than the light, for those that do evil hate the light, and will not come to the light for fear their works will be reproved.

Fear causes men to hide themselves in darkness. They fear that God may look into their hearts and see their lacks and shortcomings. But when they learn to love God, His love will help them to overcome this fear. "Perfect love casteth out fear."

Jesus told us to love God, but according to the accepted translations of the Old Testament, the prophets told us to fear God. Surely the correct interpretation of the original script in these instances must be "to revere" instead of "to fear" because Jesus spoke often of God as a loving Father, and did not speak of "fearing" God. He went so far as to point out that to love God is the first and greatest commandment. How can we both love God and be afraid of Him at the same time? We can love God and revere Him, but we cannot love and be afraid of Him.

God delivers us from evil by lovingly showing us through the teachings of Jesus how the light in us is His goodness. Jesus Christ said that He was the light of the world, and He also said: "Ye are the light of the world." The light of Christ in us will reveal to us the Truth about the one and only power in existence, and then evil will vanish out of our world as darkness vanishes before the light.

**I am open to the Father within
and I receive His love.**

A Prayer Drill

First Day. *Dear Father-God, I love You with my whole heart, soul, mind, and strength.*

Second Day. *My loving Father guides and prospers me because He loves me and I love Him.*

Third Day. *I need never be afraid of anything, because my loving Father-God is always with me. His gracious love is able to help me safely through every trial.*

Fourth Day. *When I am with the Father, He is with me.*

Fifth Day. *My Father is rich in houses and lands, but best of all, He is also rich in loving-kindness, forgiveness, joy, peace, and understanding.*

Sixth Day. *All that the Father has is mine, and all that I have is the Father's.*

Seventh Day. *My Father speaks words of life, joy, peace, courage, and love to me when I go to the secret place of the Most High in my body temple and listen to His still small voice.*

Printed in the U.S.A.

140-1653-5M-3-00